Dear Echo . . .

Dear Echo . . .

Answers to Your Questions About Ghosts,
Hauntings, and Things That Go Bump
in the Night

Echo Bodine

Thorsons

Thorsons
An Imprint of HarperCollins*Publishers*
77–85 Fulham Palace Road,
Hammersmith, London W6 8JB

The Thorsons website address is: www.thorsons.com

and *Thorsons* are trademarks of
HarperCollins*Publishers* Ltd

First published by Thorsons 2002

10 9 8 7 6 5 4 3 2 1

© Echo Bodine 2002

Echo Bodine asserts the moral right to be
identified as the author of this work

A catalogue record of this book is available
from the British Library

ISBN 0 00 714727 9

Printed and bound in USA by
R R Donnelley & Sons Company, Harrisonburg, VA

Dedication

I would like to dedicate this book
to two people I love very much

Kurt and Megan Christiansen

Acknowledgements

As always, I could have never put this book together on my own. I want to thank all of the wonderful people who went through this creation with me:

First and foremost to Susanne Sweeney who spent hours and hours categorizing and typing these great letters.

Christi Cardenas, my Agent and Guardian Angel, who spent countless hours working out all the details to make the book happen and putting up with all my "author stuff."

To my loveable (and insane) publisher Greg Brandenburgh at Thorsons/Element, whose phone calls and great sense of humor made this project so much fun.

To my editor Carolyn Pincus, book mid-wife, whose editing turned the manuscript into a book.

To Carol Lowell, Sheryl Grassie, and David Braddock for taking care of all my ghostbusting calls while I worked on the manuscript. And a special thanks to Carol Lowell for answering all the ghost mail.

To my very supportive, loving Chiropractor, Dr. Marcie New, who helped me keep my body and mind healthy, aligned and clear.

To the special people who have been very supportive while working on this project:

My mom, Mae Bodine. My boyfriend Mike Hartley, my brother Michael, my sister Nikki.

My very dear friends, Ginny Miller, Melody Beattie, Joerdie Fisher, Lorraine Roe, J. Marie Fieger, Nancy Jernander, Paula Hill.

My wonderful assistant Teri Trombley.

Contents

Things That Go Bump in the Night

*A*bout a week ago a very logical, left-brained male friend of mine called and said, "Echo, I feel like there are spirits all around me and sometimes I can see them out of the corner of my eye. The funny thing is, I never feel afraid of them. I just have the feeling I'm never alone. Are these things real or am I making this up?"

Spirits, ghosts, deceased loved ones, ghouls, specters, entities, spirit guides, angels, apparitions, poltergeists, *demons*. Yes, they are all out there and yes, they are real.

I had my first truly memorable encounter with ghosts back in 1974. I was 26 years old at the time and living on my own in an apartment in south Minneapolis. One day a friend of mine who was a psychic called to say that she'd had a strong premonition that I should move out of my place because it was no longer safe for me to live there. I completely disregarded her message. I'd lived in that apartment for over four years. It was my home, I loved it, and it had always felt perfectly safe.

About a week after she called, I came home from work to find all the drawers in my dresser pulled out and my clothes strewn all over the place. I called my landlord right away but he said he couldn't do anything for me since there were no signs of forced entry. He thought maybe I'd just forgotten to close the drawers that morning when I was getting ready for work. Yeah, right.

Later that night, after I'd gone to bed, I heard very faint mumbling voices out in my living room. I got out of bed and peeked into the room but I didn't see a thing. The noises stopped as soon as I got up. I'd been working on developing my psychic abilities for about eight years at that point, but I still wasn't able to see spirits at will or distinguish between ghosts and spirits. I would occasionally see them, but it was still hit or miss. In fact I usually saw them when I didn't want to and didn't see them when I did.

A couple of days later, I got home from work and put my key in the door. I could hear voices in my living room. I fully expected to open the door and see a group of people in there, but there was no one there. What I did find was equally disturbing. My rocking chair, which normally sat in the corner of my living room, was now in the middle of the room, rocking back and forth. I immediately called my landlord but once again, he said that since there was no forced entry into my apartment, I probably forgot that I'd left the chair in the middle of the room that morning. Yeah, right.

Later that night, just after I turned out the lights to go to sleep, the voices in the living room started up again. I didn't know what to do other than sleep with my lights on and pray for protection.

Another couple of days passed, and this time I came home from the grocery store and opened the door to find a smiley-face candle sitting in the middle of the living room floor, facing me.

I knew that candle had been on the third shelf of my bookcase when I left because that's where it always was, so needless to say, I was pretty freaked out. Only then did it dawn on me that this might be what my psychic friend was warning me about.

I called my psychic brother Michael and told him everything that was happening. I asked him if he'd spend the night with me. I figured maybe he'd hear the voices, too, and together we could figure out a solution. Of course looking back on all this today, with everything I know about ghosts, I can see the humor in it, but at the time it wasn't funny at all! Michael's girlfriend Patty came over with him and the three of us spooked each other all night with ghost stories.

With our street clothes on, we crawled under the covers of my queen sized bed and waited. It only took about five minutes before the voices started up in the living room. They were much louder this time, too. Then we all felt something step down on the bed, right by our feet. Patty and I dove under the covers. With my third eye (the spot in the middle of the forehead where psychics get their clairvoyant "pictures"), I actually saw a male spirit standing on the foot of my bed, looking down at us. He looked just like Mr. Clean, with his shiny bald head and his arms folded across his chest. And he had a look on his face that said he meant business.

My brother, who has a great sense of humor, reassured us not to worry. He crawled out from underneath the covers, saying he was going to go kick some ghost butt, and took off for the living room. We could hear him talking in a very firm voice, asking the ghosts what they wanted. Then his voice got very soft and although I could tell he was having a conversation with someone, I couldn't make out what they were saying.

After a few minutes, Michael came back into the bedroom and asked me if someone had recently told me to move. I told him about the phone call from my psychic friend but explained that I hadn't wanted to move because I loved my apartment and had no reason not to feel safe there.

He explained that the spirits he spoke with were not ghosts but just friendly spirits who were trying to get me to move out because bad things were going to start happening in the building and soon it would be unsafe for me to stay there. They told him they hadn't really wanted to scare me but didn't know any other way to get my attention. They also reassured him that now that they had accomplished what they came for, they would stop bothering me. And after that night, all the shenanigans stopped!

Well, I'll be the first to admit that I have a stubborn streak and just because three or four spirits went to all that work didn't mean I was going to start packing. Nope. I was going to stay put, especially now that the noises had stopped.

Not a week later, the boiler in the building blew up. And a week after that there was a very serious fire in the apartment two doors down from mine. No one came to my door to warn me because they thought I was at work. I only woke up when the smoke started filling my apartment. I made it to the front door, but when I opened it the smoke was so thick I couldn't see the fireman standing right in front of me. That's how bad it was. I yelled out, and that's when I realized there was someone standing just a few inches away.

The final straw came a week later when the building was broken into. I finally got the message and moved out the next month!

I share this story to show you that not all invisible visitors are malevolent, evil demons who come to do us harm. Contrary to popular belief that all ghosts or spirit activity is negative, some of the visits we experience are positive. I would say half of the spirit encounters we have are of a positive nature. Our spirit guides, deceased loved ones or guardian angels bring us news, information, comfort or advice from the other side, so it's important that we learn how to distinguish between positive and negative spirit encounters.

Since that experience at the apartment 25 years ago, I've learned a lot about ghosts and spirits. I've done countless ghost-bustings and have discovered a lot about why souls choose to remain on the earth plane rather than move on to the other side. I've also learned a great deal about how to get them to move on so that's why, in 1999, I wrote a book called *Relax, It's Only a Ghost* (Fair Winds Press). It's all about some of my real life ghost-busting adventures. Each chapter tells a different ghost story and ends with an interesting fact about ghosts. It lists the signs to look for to figure out if your house or business is haunted and has a chapter on how to get rid of a ghost.

At the back of that book, I invited readers to send me their ghost stories and questions, thinking that maybe someday down the road I'd write another book about ghosts. Well, I received so many great letters and emails that I knew I had to share them with you. The problem came in deciding which letters to include because people had such interesting stories and questions!

I enlisted my friend Susanne Sweeney to help me go through the letters and pick out 125 that seemed to best represent people's experiences, questions, and concerns. Then we put the letters into categories – real-life ghost stories, questions from teenagers about their experiences with ghosts, stories of haunted houses and possession and astral projection, questions about loved ones communicating to us through dreams, sexual encounters with ghosts – about a dozen categories in all. And that's how this book took shape.

I have changed all the names of the writers and taken out the names of the towns they live in to protect their privacy and anonymity. I have also corrected a few spelling errors and some grammar, and edited a few of the letters for length, but for the most part the letters and emails are presented to you as they were written to me. I answer all of them, although sometimes I do a "group reply" if the issues raised are similar and a single response makes the most sense.

I wrote the book to be entertaining *and* informative. We get enough goofy stuff out of Hollywood; finally here are some REAL LIFE ghost stories.

Enjoy.

Chapter One

A Ghost's Life

A ghost's life is probably not at all as you'd imagine it. I want to give you a picture of what life is really like for ghosts, so come along with me on a journey to the place where ghosts live.

I want you to imagine a very large, dark, open space filled with hundreds of thousands of souls. They look like people but many have blank stares on their faces and are so self-absorbed they aren't even aware that there are other beings floating around beside them. Even though many of them appear as if they're going somewhere, in reality they're not. They're just milling around. It's as if they're stuck in time and don't care. There's no happiness in this place. No sense of life or purpose. They look like a bunch of zombies, floating around in a state of confusion or purposely avoiding the future.

These are not highly evolved souls. They're what we call level one and two souls, which means they are still in the earliest stages of developing a consciousness about life or death or them-selves. Many have no belief in God or spirituality. Others believe

1

in a judgmental, punishing, condemning deity who is anxiously waiting to send them to hell for their sins. They don't know about spirit guides or guardian angels and are suspicious that anyone who might come to "take them home" is simply the Devil in disguise.

Many are quite confused about life after death while others are aware of what's going on and know they could move on to Heaven but choose to remain in this place of nothingness. Some believe death is simply a vacuum of emptiness, and rather than reach out to others for help with their plight, they simply choose to stay stuck. They prefer to hold on to their former lives and identity. Many are filled with self-pity, anger, resentments, fear, or self-loathing. They wander this place staying stuck in time and avoiding change. This vast wasteland of nothingness is called the Astral Plane and many souls choose to live here after their physical body dies.

From where they are, every one of them can see a beautiful light glowing at the "front door" of the other side. They all see the road that leads to the other side and many times a day see souls making that journey into the light, but for their various reasons none of these souls wants anything to do with that place. Some believe that if they even try to go there, God will snatch them up and send them straight to hell. Others are afraid to go for fear that they'll run into people they don't want to see. Some don't believe they have a right to go to Heaven and others don't believe in a Heaven and think this special road actually leads to Hell. They refuse to go in case they're being tricked. The majority of them simply want to hang on to who they *were* and not move on.

There are other souls in this place as well. There are souls who have committed suicide and are afraid to take the road home for fear they won't be allowed in or will be sent to Hell for the "sin" of taking their own life. There are souls who were addicted to things of the physical body such as food, alcohol, drugs and sex who aren't ready to let go of their addictions. They hang out in this vast wasteland hoping to find a way to continue to get high or experience their addiction.

How Houses Become Haunted

Now I want you to imagine that this vast wasteland is the next dimension just above the Earth plane. These stuck souls can see our homes, businesses, schools, and all the *people* still living on Earth. Sometimes they get lonely, bored or restless and decide to look around for some action. And that's when they become ghosts – when they come to Earth and make themselves known to us through their antics. Even though most of them are loners and rarely socialize, many are drawn to houses that have other earth-bound spirits in them because they like knowing there are others around just like them. This is how a home becomes haunted.

It gets even more interesting. Earthbound spirits who were addicts in life will look around for the home of an addict with the same addiction so that they can enter the addict's body (more on this in Chapter 5, Possession and Astral Projection) and continue to experience their preferred high. This is one way a person becomes possessed.

At some point, the more advanced earthbound spirits realize they can manipulate energy and because they get bored or get a kick out of frightening people, some of them might start playing tricks to get people's attention. If your lights, TV or radio go on and off, it's a safe bet that it's one of these ansy earthbound spirits. They learn that fear and anger are two powerful emotions that create a lot of energy, so they'll try to create these emotions by frightening people. Then they'll either breathe in this energy to boost their own energy or use it to make more scary things happen, which then generates more energy, etc. etc.

People living in haunted houses often know that something isn't right but they don't know how to interpret what's happening or what to do about it. They might *see* something wispy or floating out of the corner of their eye but then chalk it up to an overactive imagination or something they saw on television. They may *feel* afraid but they don't take it seriously and that gets the ghosts feeling even more rambunctious. That's usually when ghosts will begin tapping on the walls or making footstep sounds or pulling the clothes out of closets. Or moving things from room to room, jangling door knobs, turning wastebaskets upside down, manipulating someone's alarm clock to go off at a different time, tipping things over, making mumbling sounds. They might walk through you, giving you the feeling of a cold breeze whooshing through your body. All of this to get a rise out of people with the hope of sucking up their fear energy.

You can tell when an earthbound spirit possesses a substance addict, because the addict will act as if they've gone through some kind of personality change. They'll do things that are out of character for them. Then, they'll wake up from being high and "not feel like themselves." Their loved ones will see a change in their personality. It's the eyes that give them away. If you look into the eyes of a possessed person, the eyes of a stranger will stare back at you.

When a sex addict is inhabited by a sex-addicted ghost, the ghost will try to get them to do things they would never otherwise do. They'll have sexual thoughts that they've never had before or do things that are out of character. People who have sex with a spouse possessed by a sex-addicted ghost can usually tell that something's not right. They feel as if they're having sex with a stranger but because they don't know how to interpret the personality change, the spouse often thinks there's something wrong with *them!*

These stories are *real,* my friends. This is what ghosts are really about. They are angry, stuck, miserable, rebellious, lonely, depressed, afraid of God and/or formerly addicted souls. They are lost. Many don't want to accept that they've died and almost all of them do not want to move on.

In their opinion, the next best thing to being alive is to hang out here with us on the Earth plane, and they'll do almost anything to get our attention. I've rarely met a ghost who doesn't eventually get bored being all alone and want some kind of contact. They'll look for a home inhabited by other ghosts, but they'll also look for homes that have sensitive (psychic) people in them. They can tell this by looking at our auras (the energy around our bodies). The colors and the intensity of the colors tells them which members of the household will respond to them the best.

For example, intellectuals' auras tend to have a lot of yellow in them. Ghosts usually stay away from people with yellow auras because they learn early on that intellectuals are always looking for rational explanation for everything and they can't get a rise out of them. It's a waste of energy. So if they see a yellow aura, they'll just move on.

On the other hand, people with pink in their auras are very sensitive and would be open to having psychic experiences. Ghosts who can find a teenager with pink in their aura feel like they've hit the jackpot because teenagers are almost always more open to having "ghostly encounters" and less likely to tell the spirits to get lost.

The double bonus for the ghost comes when the sensitive person buys himself a Ouija Board, because now the ghost has a surefire way of communicating with them. They'll have a constant audience for their antics.

The Difference Between Ghosts and Spirits

There are basically two kinds of spirits: souls who remain earth-bound, which we call ghosts, and souls who move on to the other side or Heaven, which are commonly referred to as spirits. Spirits will visit us on Earth, but they will always go home again to the other side.

Ghosts and spirits will both appear just as they did in their last life, which can make it pretty confusing to tell who's who. The giveaway, usually, is that ghosts tend to have an unhappy look to them whereas spirits seem almost to glow. A ghost will usually seem depressed or irritable, with a certain blankness to his face, like the lights are on but no one's home. His aura is usually grayish and you always get the feeling that he's got unfinished business. Spirits, on the other hand, tend to look radiant. Within a couple of weeks of crossing over, they appear younger looking, with no signs of stress on their face. Being with them you sense that they are looking forward to resting and healing from their recent life experience. They're happy to be reunited with loved ones and radiate a sense of anticipation about their new life.

There are souls coming and going all the time in the Astral Plane and you can tell by their energy, aura or appearance who are the stuck souls and who are the free spirits.

What to Do with a Stuck Soul

People often ask me how can they tell whether they're being visited by a deceased love one or are housing a ghost. It's usually pretty easy to tell. You'd rarely feel *comforted* by a ghost, but a loved one will almost always make you feel comforted in her presence. Our loved ones also usually send us clues that they're around – they project a thought of themselves to us or send us a smell we'd immediately associate with them, like their cologne.

It's important to remember that stuck souls have not been abandoned here or forgotten by unstuck souls. They *choose* to hang around. In fact, spirits are always crossing over from the other side to try to convince ghosts to come home (see the section on the Squadron in my Solutions chapter). Sometimes they succeed, but sometimes they don't. The point is, we all have free will in death just as we do in life and God doesn't make any of us do anything. If a soul wants to hang around the astral plane, that's his or her choice.

That said, there *are* things we can do on this side to help them cross over. The most useful thing we can do is put our foot down and demand that they move on. Many times all they need is a push, a stern voice telling them they are not welcome and that they have to leave *now* and go to the white light. That may seem too easy, but trust me, it really works.

Now that you have a clearer picture of what ghosts and spirits are really about, I'd like to share some of the letters I've received. As you read what people have written and my responses, you'll get lots more insight into the world of ghosts, as well as some practical tips on what to do to get them to move on.

Chapter Two

Letters from Teenagers

*E*ver since I published *Relax, It's Only a Ghost,* I have received dozens of letters from teenagers. As I explained in the introduction, teenagers are particularly vulnerable to ghosts and spirits because they're naturally more open and curious. But they can also be more isolated and freaked out by their experiences with ghosts, so I always try to answer their letters and give them a little guidance or at least reassurance that they're not going crazy.

When I hear from a young person I'm always reminded of my own early days as a psychic. I was 17 years old and a very impressionable teenager when I was first told by a medium that I had psychic abilities. I had gone for my first psychic reading with Eve Olson, a medium from England, and she told me that I had two spirit guides watching over me. I remember the feeling like it was yesterday. I was comforted by the idea that I had spirit guides but also pretty nervous. I wondered if they were around me all the time and if they knew my every thought and deed. Were they watching me get dressed? Were they with me in the bathroom?

I was constantly looking for a sign of their presence. If a light bulb flickered or the house creaked, I would wonder if they were trying to contact me. If anything in my room was out of place, I figured they had moved it to get my attention. I remember spending many slumber parties with my girlfriends, with us all scared out of our wits at the thought that spirits were trying to communicate with us.

I had a lot of the same experiences that these teenagers have had: I can remember feeling a negative presence in my room or other parts of the house, sensing someone watching me, hiding under my covers at night for fear of seeing something. I remember seeing a head floating in the hallway one night and another time seeing a man, though only from the waist up, standing at the end of my bed. (My psychic development teacher later explained that it wasn't uncommon to see only a portion of a spirit because some spirits have a limited amount of energy and therefore can only make a portion of themselves visible).

Sometimes I would feel a cold energy move through my body. Candles would blow out all by themselves. I would hear mumbling voices but could never make out any specific words. Sometimes the spirits would move the needle on my record player (some of you probably don't even know what that is!) and sometimes they'd change the channel on the television set (this was before the invention of the remote control, if you can believe that). Flickering lights, heads walking down the hall, mumbling voices – no wonder I was half scared out of my wits and slept with the lights on every night.

To make matters worse, against the advice of our psychic teacher, Birdie, my mom and I decided to buy a Ouija Board. Bringing that Board into the house was one of the stupidest things we've ever done. Talk about opening up to the spirit world! It was insanity. But we loved to ask questions and watch that little "thingy" (the planchette) move around the Board and spell out messages. We would consult that Board on a daily basis.

Birdie had warned us not to play with it until we were better at seeing spirits and could determine who we were communicating with, but to us not knowing made it even more exciting. To be perfectly honest, we were drama junkies. We loved to be scared and excited and the Board provided all that and *more*.

After a while, though, the Board started spelling out really negative, menacing messages. It would tell us that we were going to be killed in car accidents or we were going to get really sick and die – things like that. We had opened ourselves up to the fun and excitement of communicating with spirits, but the spirits we were attracting were far from positive. They would tell us they were high spiritual beings and that they worked for God, but their messages were getting more and more negative and we eventually had to get rid of the Board.

I'll never forget the night we finally decided we'd had enough. We were all sitting around the dinner table and we could hear voices calling my name in a very sickly tone of voice. "Echo, Echo, come here." "Echo, Echo, come here." We were pretty scared. My mom called Birdie and she said that the voices were coming from the spirits attracted to the Ouija Board and that they wanted us to play the Board because they had a message for us. She told mom to burn the Board in the fireplace and never to play with another one again. But we were so addicted to it that the thought of burning it seemed cruel, so mom took it out to the garbage. The next morning when we came down to breakfast, the Board was sitting on the kitchen table! Needless to say, we burned it that day.

Looking back on all the scary experiences we had with that Board, I understand what my teacher meant when she said to stay away from Ouija Boards until we knew what we were doing. Here's my advice to any of you out there who think it would be fun to mess around with the Ouija Board or call in spirits or try to read people's futures: find something else to be passionate about for now. You can always get into this after you've studied the paranormal and have a better idea of what you're dealing with.

Over the last thirty years, I've received numerous phone calls and letters from teenagers or their parents asking if I would teach them how to develop their psychic abilities and my inner voice has always said a resounding NO, not at this vulnerable time in their life. To those of you wanting to develop your psychic abilities, I just want to say not now. You're going through enough changes in your life. You're still trying to figure out who you are, you've got intense peer pressure, you're going through hormonal changes, your relationships with your parents are changing. You're trying to figure out about dating, possibly exploring your sexuality, getting a job for the first time, making decisions about your future regarding education and goals. There's so much stimulus in your life; opening up psychically will only complicate things for you. Don't worry. If in a few years you're still interested in developing your abilities, they'll still be there for you to work with. Just please wait until you've gotten more life experience. You really don't want to open this can of worms until you know how to deal with the worms.

Okay, so let's look at some of those letters:

Dear Echo,

Hi, my name is Amy. I am 13 years old. Ever since I can remember I have been able to predict the future and get extremely strong feelings about spirits. Usually when I get afraid I'll pray to God to send down my Grandmother who died when I was six. I can feel her with me. I'll give her a spot to sit on my bed and I'll fall asleep to the songs she'll sing to me or the stories she'll tell. I don't always have to pray for my grandma, though. In fact most of the time she'll just show up when I need her. It's not always at my house either. She will frequently visit me at school or when I'm with a friend.

And it's also not always my grandmother. Sometimes it's my dog or other relatives. My great-grandfather died in front of me about 2 months ago. Since then, I have been feeling something with a negative energy in my bedroom. It may be my grandfather, but he was always so kind and loving. Why would he have a negative energy? But the energy is not the worst part. The worst part is that usually when I am not at ease I pray for my grandma to come down and calm me down. Now when I do so she doesn't come. And as each day passes I grow more fearful of entering my room because I don't know who the negative spirit is.

As I approach my room I get this cold, prickly feeling running down my back and fingers. Once I'm inside my heart begins to beat very hard and very fast. I always grab my neck too because I can feel something touching it.

These days I fall asleep very cold and frightened. I hide my head under the covers to try and hide myself from the spirit. Night after night I have nightmares. I usually enjoy talking to spirits but not this one. I think my grandma doesn't like the spirit either and that's why she won't come down to talk to me anymore. Another *weird thing: my bird always bites me when I try to get her into her cage, which is in my room. That never used to happen. And I have to change my light bulb at least twice a week. Is there anything you can tell me that may help me to get rid of this scary spirit?*

I thank you so much for your time,

Amy

Dear Amy:

I can assure you that the negative energy in your room is not your grandma or grandpa. Sometimes when we ask our deceased loved ones to come and be with us, they're busy and not able to come right away, but that doesn't mean they don't love us anymore, it simply means they're busy doing something else. Here's an example of a time my grandma did come when I asked her to, but also explained that it wouldn't happen every time.

Several years ago I was seeing a psychiatrist for depression. He did not believe in psychic abilities or any of the other things I believed in. One day he told me that I needed to forget all this business and get on with my life. He said "if there really are spirits, have someone come here and prove it to me." Silently I called out to my grandma, who had been deceased for some time. About fifteen seconds later, she came into the room and asked me what was up. I told her that this doctor didn't believe in spirits and asked her if there was anything she could do to convince him.

She walked right over to him and put her hands on his neck. She told me she didn't like this guy and that he wouldn't be much help to me regarding the depression. The doctor started squirming in his chair and asked me if something was standing behind him.

I told him my grandmother was standing behind him with her hands on his neck and he got up from his chair and moved to the front side of his desk. He asked me to tell her to go away. Before she left, my grandma explained to me that she had a life going on on the other side, and that there would be times she wouldn't be able to come when I asked her to. She said it didn't mean she didn't love me, it just meant that she was very busy doing something.

About the scary presence in your room, you have to put your foot down and demand that it leave. You should never be frightened to go into your own room. You can ask an angel to come in and protect you and ask it to clear your room of any negative presences or energy. Angels are very efficient with this, so it should work just fine.

A good indicator will be your bird. Our pets are very sensitive to any kind of spirit activity. Sounds like your bird isn't feeling very safe right now either which is another reason why you should put your foot down and demand that the ghost leave *now!*

Sincerely,

Echo

Dear Echo,

Hi, my name is Karrie and I need your help. I don't know what I am or what I have psychically, but I know I am constantly afraid. When my mom was alive she always encouraged me to develop my gifts but now she has passed on to her next life. I am still afraid and constantly trying to shut everything off. I can see auras and could probably be a medium. I feel like I'm being watched all the time. I really want to develop my abilities but I have a feeling that I need a guide because it could be dangerous. I haven't ever contacted my guide because I'm afraid of what I might find out. I was hoping that you could help me in some way. I am reading Relax, It's Only a Ghost *and I only wish things would happen to me like you explain in your book about people contacting you and helping you.*

Thank you for your time, I really hope to hear from you.

Sincerely,

Karrie

Dear Karrie:

I would suggest that you check your area for any new age or alternative bookstores. Call and ask if they know of any reputable psychic teachers you could contact. If there are none available, check your yellow pages for a local Unity church. They may know of a reputable psychic who teaches classes. You need a good teacher to help you work with your gifts and help you heal your fears. A class is a great place to start.

If you're not able to find a teacher after calling a bookstore or a Unity church, perhaps the timing isn't right. There's an old saying, "when the student is ready, the teacher will appear." Just be patient and trust the wisdom of the Universe. It will bring you your teacher when you're ready.

In the meantime, find things of this world to become interested in. This might sound like it has nothing to do with being psychic, but having a creative hobby is great for helping you feel grounded, and being grounded is an important part of developing your psychic abilities. Please try to be patient and don't push yourself to develop your abilities now.

I would also suggest journaling about your fears. Journaling can really help you heal. It will all come together at some point. Listen to your intuition and you will be guided as to what to do next. If you're not sure how to listen to your intuition, you might want to get a copy of my book *A Still Small Voice; A Psychic's Guide to Awakening Intuition.* That will also be an excellent tool to lay the foundation for your psychic development.

Sincerely,

Echo

Earthbound spirits love to mess with teenagers because they can pretty much count on a reaction. As you'll see from the following four letters, they usually aren't doing any real harm. They're just doing the usual prankster-type gags to scare these young girls. Because all four letters raise similar issues, I did a "group reply." Here goes:

Dear Ms. Bodine,

Hello, my name is Kathy and I am 15 years old. I am writing to see if maybe you could help me. For about the past year things have been happening to me. I have seen and heard things that I cannot explain. Here are a few examples of what's been going on:

1) The biggest thing is that I have been hearing people talking. I am the only one who can hear them. Sometimes it's just mumbling, and others it's full out conversations. You might think it's my house or something but I hear things in other places too.

2) Sometimes when I close my eyes I see images. Twice I have seen these white, hazy mist things. One time I was lying in my bed with my eyes closed and there floating above me was a mist. Another time I actually saw one floating in my room.

3) The scariest image I have seen was of a man with a gun. I was just going to sleep and I had already been hearing a mumbling conversation. I closed my eyes and a few seconds later

I saw a man with a gun walk through my door, actually through my door. (I can't sleep with doors open.) The conversation I heard became very heated, there was a silence, and a bang!

4) There are other things, like my TV will either switch channels by itself or turn itself off. I've heard breathing other than my own, I've heard footsteps outside my room, (I am very sensitive to movement and sound) I can hear people walking in my hall with the door closed. I can also sense when and sometimes even who is outside my door before they walk into the room.

I appreciate you taking time out to read this, and I would really, really like you to e-mail me back, as soon as possible please. If you need me to I can e-mail you more information about myself. Thank you.

Kathy

Dear Echo,

Hi, I'm only 15 and need some serious help. I can predict things, once I saw a ghost, twice I've tried to talk to them, and always get chills or goose bumps, hear strange noises, and weird visions. At first I thought I was like a witch or something, but I'm not pagan, I'm Catholic. I've tried everything, but your book seemed to help.

What do you do when you know there's a ghost in the house but you can't see or hear it? You just get weird feelings and know they're there?

I know that a few of my friends have the same problems! Is everyone psychic and just some more than others or what? Or is it just the few who believe? Can you help?

Thank you, many questions, no answers.

Echo,

This is Marty. I'm 12 and from Minnesota.

I have ghosts in my house. My best friend has them, too. How do I know I have ghosts? Well my mom and I have seen them. When my mom had her bed on the same wall as the door and her dresser/mirror angled so that you could see out the doorway at night, we saw shadow people walking past. We hear weird noises sometimes and when me and my friend were checking to see if they were real or not we heard music.

Another time when I had a sleepover we did the Ouija Board in our guest room. We were contacting the ghosts and my friend yelled at them and they threw a shoe at her and missed and hit our TV. We all ran into my room and they came pounding on the door. When we tried to light a candle it kept blowing out. I've gotten used to it. I'm not scared anymore but they still bother me.

But this is the mother of all ghost stories that have happened in my house: one night I was brushing my teeth in the bathroom. I had the door partway open. Everyone in the house was asleep and all of a sudden I felt a breeze go by and I heard giggling. I was so scared. I followed your advice and used a whole can of air freshener on them and they got scared of it and went away for a few days. Do you have any suggestions of what they might want? Please help.

Marty

Hi, my name is Kirsten. I'm 13 years old. I live in MN. I'm having problems with my ghosts and it's starting to scare me. I really need your help. My parents won't believe me but my best friend is helping through this. She has one of your books. She thinks you're cool. She tried that one method to get rid of them *[with the air freshener] and it helped. We are trying to find time to do it at my house but in the meantime I need your advice. This is what they have done in the past few days:*

1. I was watching TV and my closet door started to open.

2. I went upstairs to get a drink and when I came back my TV was on a different channel.

3. The bathroom door slammed shut for no reason.

4. Half the kitchen blinds were turned upside down.

I don't know what it all means so if you have any ideas I would like you to share them with me. Thanks a ton!

Sincerely,

Kirsten

Dear Kathy, Marty, Kirsten, and friend:

As I mentioned earlier, ghosts are not exactly highly evolved souls. Because they choose not to move on to the other side, they have lots of time on their hands, so many of them will go looking for sensitive people to spook. They like scaring people. They probably did similar things when they were living and this is how they get their kicks now that they're dead.

The best thing you can do with ghosts like yours is to be very firm. Tell them they *must* go on to the other side, and if they don't want to, they must leave your house *NOW!*

You don't have to do this by yourself. You can call in all kinds of help. There are wonderful angels that will always help out when asked, but you do need to ask. They won't interfere in your life. But all you have to do is ask for a healing angel to come in and cleanse your house of anything negative and they will come.

The other helpers you can call on are a group called the Squadron. They are a bunch of spirits who used to be ghosts and

19

have now moved on to the other side. If you call on them, they will gladly come and help out. Just ask out loud that the Squadron (see Solutions) please come and clear your home of any unwanted ghosts or negative presences and it will be done.

The other suggestion, which one of you tried successfully, is to get a can of air freshener and spray the ghosts when you sense their presence or when they start doing their little tricks to try to frighten you. Spray it right at them or in the direction you believe they are in and tell them to go to the white light. I'm not exactly sure why this works, but I've gotten several letters back from people who tried it and said it worked very well.

Above all else, remember that these ghosts love to get a rise out of people. That's what all the fun is about for them, so try not to react. If you don't react, if you find other things to do besides focus on them, after a while they'll get bored and move on.

Sincerely,

Echo

This next letter reminds me of the movie *The Sixth Sense* and a common myth about ghosts. All of the ghosts in that movie appear as they did at the time of their death, and some appeared as if they had blood on them. Some people believe that all ghosts are here because they don't know they're dead, but that's not true. A small percentage of ghosts that are roaming around don't know they are dead, and the give-away for me always is how they appear when I first see them. If they appear as if they've just died, with blood still on their clothing or in a hospital gown, that usually tells me they don't know they're dead.

Ghosts appear to us as they think of themselves. If they think of themselves in blue jeans and a shirt, that's how we'll see them.

I once encountered a ghost named Kenneth who didn't know he was dead. He appeared to me in his soldier's uniform (he had fought in Viet Nam), with a big, bloody bullet hole in him. Kenneth hadn't moved on mentally. He continued to think of himself as a soldier and that's why he appeared in a bloody uniform.

When this next girl first saw her ghost, the ghost had blood on her clothing, but then the next time she saw her the blood was gone. This tells me the ghost wasn't mentally stuck at her death.

Dear Echo Bodine,

Hi, I am 12 years old and going into the 7th grade. I wanted to tell you some of my ghost stories.

One night I couldn't fall asleep for nothing. It was about 2:00 in the morning and I was just looking around my room. Then I saw a ghost. She was facing the wall and wearing ripped clothes. I could see that she was bleeding (blood was pouring down her head). I was so scared. I hid underneath the covers. Then I fell asleep. When I woke up I looked to see if she was still there. She was. She appeared to be wearing a dress (gown), but now she wasn't bleeding, she was smiling. I was scared to death!

Another time was I sleeping with my mom. When I looked over at her side of the bed there was an old man staring at me in an angry face. As always, I hid underneath the covers waiting for it to go away. Other times I would see a shadow of a little girl walking in my living room. Or feel cold breezes walk past me. Sometimes I get really hot and then I get chills.

I don't know what to do, I don't want to talk to them. I am scared! What do you think they want from me? What should I do? How could I keep these ghosts away?

P.S. Write back please? I want to be friends with you.

Sherrie

21

Dear Sherrie:

A lot of my teenage correspondents ask what the ghosts want from them. Truth be told, for a lot of these ghosts their only agenda is scaring us! They don't come with some important message from the great beyond. Heck, they haven't even gone over to the great beyond yet! They're just biding time and hoping to find someone to spook.

As I always advise, call in the helpers to clear out your house, then ask your guides to protect your house from any more ghost invaders, and try to get on with your life.

It's important to remember that you have to *really* want them gone, or they won't leave. They can sense our intentions. If you're kind of passive, wishy washy, and "kind of" ask them to leave, they're not going to go away! Or they might leave temporarily but come back. If you really want them to go, you have to stay firm and demand that they leave you alone, and they'll leave and stay gone. The outcome really is up to you.

Good luck.

Sincerely,

Echo

Ms. Echo Bodine,

I'm a 16-year-old from Wisconsin and I work at a restaurant that's haunted by a ghost. One of the women I work with gave me your book Relax, It's Only a Ghost *because I've been pretty freaked out about it.*

In the 1930s the woman who owned this restaurant fell down the basement stairs drunk. The people who work here all agree that her soul hangs around to help protect the owning family and the employees from falling like she did.

Last March, I happened to be the first person to see her. She was on the stairs leading to the basement. Books I've read have said kids are more likely to see spirits. My friend and I are the only kids who work there. Anyway, after I saw this ghost I refused to go downstairs alone. Since then ghosts have been my biggest fear.

I'm writing to see if you've any suggestions on how to calm my fear. I've told the ghost I don't mind its presence and to please go about its business when I'm not there. All the other employees like having the ghost there. I'm not actually scared of her, just the thought of it being there. Any suggestions would be greatly appreciated.

Sincerely,

Patty

Dear Patty:

My experience tells me your ghost isn't hanging around to protect others. As I was reading your letter, I got the feeling that she's actually quite self-absorbed and loves all the attention she gets.

There is something you can do to calm your fears, though. Tell her that you don't want her to appear to you anymore. Then ask your guides to protect you from seeing any spirits.

As far as ghost pictures go, if you have access to the Internet, go to my website, www.echobodine.com, from time to time and check out the links. When my webmaster finds cool ghost links he lists them on my site.

Sincerely,

Echo

Echo,

Hello. My name is Vicky. I am 16 years old. I've only had one run-in with a ghost in my entire life. It was three or four years ago and it was kind of cool. It was a friend of mine's great-grandmother. We were in her basement about a month after she died. We were in the farthest room back in the house and we turned to leave the room and the door slammed shut and locked. Then this greenish hazy glow appeared and we saw a face begin to form. It was the only part of her that actually got definition to it. She only stayed for a minute and then she vanished. The door unlocked and reopened. That was the last time I actually saw a ghost.

There was a particular story in your book that I really enjoyed – the one about the bar in Kentucky. I was wondering what it feels like when you have to deal with a very angry ghost, and do you ever feel sad when you encounter small children spirits? Thank you for your time. I'm sure you are very busy, but I would be very grateful if you responded to my letter.

Sincerely,

Vicky

Dear Vicky:

Running into angry ghosts or children ghosts is just like running into angry people or small children in life. What has always seemed odd to me is that I frequently run into young ghosts who aren't accompanied by an adult. They *are* usually in groups, though, so I guess I shouldn't worry about them.

Angry ghosts are a different matter. You know that bar in Kentucky that you mentioned in your letter? Well, I went back down there a second time because the A&E channel wanted to do a follow-up story on it. The second time I encountered a new ghost named Buck. He was one mean dude. According to the bouncer, this ghost broke a beer bottle on his head and he had to have 20 stitches to sew it up. He was a big guy in life and appeared big as a ghost also. He just stood there, looking mean. I think he thought he was really cool.

Anyway, he told me he killed his brother with his bare hands. I don't know if the story was true or not, but one thing was perfectly clear. There was no way this guy was interested in going to the light. He *wanted* to hang around that bar all day and cause problems. I tried talking to him about going over to the other side, but he wanted nothing to do with it, so I just had to let him be.

So, in answer to your question, dealing with angry spirits is just like dealing with angry people. It isn't pleasant.

Sincerely,

Echo

Whether you're thirteen or thirty, one thing you need to remember is that you are more powerful than any ghost. If you don't want to see ghosts, put your foot down and tell them to stop bothering you and move on to the other side. Tell them to look for the white light and go to it *now*. Don't treat them like they're scary monsters because they aren't monsters. They're simply souls who have chosen to stay earthbound. Unfortunately they get their kicks from messing with people, especially vulnerable teenagers. You can get rid of them, but you *really have to want them gone.*

When I was a kid, anytime our house seemed overrun with spirits, my mom would call this guy we had met at a psychic convention and he would come over and get rid of them. He always did a great job. The scary noises and spooky experiences would stop. The problem was that life would get so quiet and *normal* that we would start missing our ghosts and want them back. Of course back they'd come, each time bringing more ghosts with them.

I can assure you, you have the power to get rid of any spirits who might be roaming the halls of your home. You can close that door to the spirit world and you won't be bothered anymore, if and when you decide you're done.

Chapter Three

When the Psychically
Gifted See Ghosts

*M*ost of the letters I receive from people about having a ghost in their home are not as clearly defined as these next few letters, simply because most people haven't developed their psychic abilities. I wanted to share these stories with you so that you could see some of the ghost stories through the eyes of psychically gifted people. In this first letter, for instance, the writer describes seeing pictures of ghosts as a movie in her head, which is exactly how clairvoyance works. We all have a third eye, located in the middle of our forehead, and this is what sees images, visions or "movies," as the writer calls them.

She also talks about ghosts traveling from one house to the next, which is actually not very common. Ghosts are notorious for not wanting any change in their lives and often when a family is getting ready to move, instead of going with the family, the ghost may try to prevent the family from leaving.

I remember this one ghostbusting job I went on several years ago. The ghost really liked the family that lived in the house and did not want them to move. So what he would do is stand by the front door and wait for the realtor to bring by prospective buyers. As soon as the people would approach the door, the ghost would literally walk through them, sending a chilling sensation of cold wind through their body. The realtor couldn't understand what was happening. She told the family that a lot of people really liked the look of the house from the outside but would get to the door and not even want to go in.

The owners called me in after the house had been on the market for several months because they couldn't find any logical reason for the house not selling. When I approached the front door I immediately saw the problem. A male ghost was standing in the entryway. He saw me looking at him and darted up the stairs. When I caught up with him, I asked him what was going on and he told me that he really liked this family and didn't want to take a chance on another family moving in that he might not like. After I spent close to an hour trying to convince him to go to the other side, he finally gave in and went. The house sold within a week.

This next letter also points out that ghosts don't like change. When the writer and her daughter spent the night at a friend's house and slept in his bed, his ghost wasn't too happy about it. As you'll see, ghosts are real creatures of habit and will often get pretty noisy in response to change.

Dear Ms. Bodine,

My name is Nora. I'm 28 and a Medical Assistant. Since I was a child, I've heard voices when no one was there and seen dark, shadowy figures walking down the hallway and around my room. I was brought up to believe that there are no such things as a soul and that when you died, you died – that's it. I was taught that it was demons that haunted people in the dark. I never really accepted those beliefs, and as soon as I was on my own, I started reading about the supernatural and the occult and meeting like-minded people. Anyway, at the end of your book, you invited people to tell you their ghost stories. Here are some of mine.

An old friend of mine's mom committed suicide when he was little. It messed him up pretty badly. One day he decided that he wanted to visit her grave. He hadn't visited in years. I went with him to the cemetery but when we got there he didn't know exactly where her gravesite was. I was maybe twenty feet away when I decided to take matter into my own hands. I closed my eyes, relaxed, and asked where she was. A sudden, soft breeze picked up and lead me right to the grave. The stone was the flat kind in the ground and it was covered with dirt and leaves. My friend couldn't believe I'd found it. While he went to get water to clean the stone, I sat on her grave and cursed her out for being so stupid and selfish and messing up her son.

Then I started seeing this movie in my head. It seemed to go on for a long time but it really lasted only an instant. Anyway, in the movie his mother was driving a reddish-orange station wagon and following a man. Then I saw her as a little girl holding hands with another little girl. They had on little white dresses and brown, buckled, leather shoes and they were climbing up some stone steps to a white house.

That night I told my friend about my vision and that I thought his mom had committed suicide because of a man. He couldn't believe it. I then described her sister and the house. He was shocked because I didn't even know she had a sister and the house I described was his grandmother's. I scared him so much that he made me turn the lights on!

Another time I spent the night at a friend's house with my daughter. My friend told me that he has a family of ghosts that travel with him from house to house. My daughter and I slept on his bed while he slept downstairs. All night long we could hear someone walking up and down the creaky hallway and around the bed. At one point I looked up and saw a tall shadow of a man walking down the hallway. My daughter sat up, wide awake from a deep sleep, and looked right at him and said, "go to sleep, you're making too much noise!" I then went downstairs and woke up my friend and told him that one of his ghosts wouldn't let us sleep because he didn't know who we were. As soon as my friend joined us, the ghost left us alone.

Once, another friend of mine's aunt passed away unexpectedly in her sleep. We went over to her house that day. We were gathered around the kitchen when I saw her. I leaned over to my friend and asked him if his aunt stood in the corner of the kitchen when commanding attention. He said she did. I then described her to a tee, used phrases and words she used, and told my friend that his aunt was angry at the way people were acting because it was making her husband sadder. She then moved to her husband's side and stayed there.

Another time I was visiting with a girlfriend of mine and she began to reminisce about her grandpa. She and her family are from Kuwait. As soon as she started talking I could see her grandfather by her side. I described him, again using phrases and words he used. I then heard him speaking French. I didn't understand him but I knew it was French and I could tell he was using endearments. When I told my friend she got misty eyed.

Her grandpa spoke fluent French and would always say sweet things to her like that.

By the way, when I "see" ghosts or spirits it's with my mind, not my eyes. When they speak to me, I hear their voices in my head. This doesn't happen to me a lot and sometimes I only feel a presence but don't see or hear anything. Is it sometimes like this for you?

I hope you enjoyed my stories. I've been told I have spirit guides but they sit back and are silent because I haven't acknowledged them yet. I've tried and I do meditate but I haven't met them yet. Any suggestions?

Dear Nora:

After reading your letter, I don't think you need to be too concerned about not being able to communicate with your spirit guides. From all the experiences you've shared with me, it's pretty clear that you have psychic abilities and I would guess it's just a matter of time before you see and hear them like you do these ghosts. Besides being impressed with your abilities, I also like the fact that you don't seem afraid of any of these spirits, earthbound or otherwise.

I would suggest keeping a journal of all your psychic experiences because it's been my experience that the memories fade over time and you'll want to remember the insights you gained from each experience. It will also help you gain confidence in your psychic abilities. My sense is that you'll definitely be using your gifts to help family and friends deal with the loss of their loved ones. If you ever decide to become a ghostbuster, let me know.

Sincerely,

Echo

Here is another letter from a psychically gifted writer. I wish everyone was as tuned into their surroundings as this young woman:

Dear Ms. Bodine,

I have lived with the spirit world all my life. I must admit that I have never had a ghost throw something at me or make life difficult. I have always had a good relationship with the ghosts/spirits around me.

I have heard the voices of spirits from a very early age. I have never doubted that the spirit world exists because my spirit guides and other forms of ghosts/spirits have helped me through very difficult times in my life. They even helped me with my ultimate choice of mate.

The ghosts I have known were usually family, but I also knew a cranky old farmer in Connecticut who made our garage door open and shut. He also banged around a bit. Our house was new but sat on the spot where his house used to be. I was only five at the time, but he seemed nice enough. I must admit that I missed him when we moved.

The story I wish to tell you, however, is about my maternal grand-mother. I never really knew her when she was alive. She died when I was only four and my memories of her are very limited. I know that she was a very dynamic woman and died a slow and painful death. She died relatively young. She smoked and had very bad emphysema and she was addicted to narcotic pills. Ultimately she died of a heart attack. My mother tells me that she was talking about or to me the day she died. I was not at the hospital, but I heard her.

When I was thirteen my parents suffered a financial setback and we had to move into my grandfather's house. I had never visited my grandfather at his home until that time. Everyone told stories about the odd things that occurred in that house, but I did not believe them until I moved in. Immediately I began to sense a presence, sometimes very strongly. It was clear that the presence disturbed everyone in the house but grandfather and me. My father always felt ill at ease. My mother became difficult and hard to live with. My brother could not get out of the house fast enough. We lived there for three years and I became very attached to the house and the presence. I found it comforting and loving.

When I was twenty I moved back into my grandfather's house because it was close to the college I was attending. All my cousins and both of my brothers had attempted to live with grandfather, but they were so uncomfortable in the house that they could not stay. None of them lasted there more than a month.

To everyone's surprise, I loved living there. I cared for the house, the garden, the lawn, and the errands. I took grandfather anywhere he wanted to go. I was a music major and he loved to hear me practice. Grandfather was very happy with the arrangement and apparently so was grandmother. I never saw her, but I knew she was there. I was the only grandchild to live with grandfather successfully.

Interestingly enough, I felt the presence in the house very strongly. I would often "hear" the various sounds that everyone reported, such as my grandmother's old stair lift going up and down or footsteps upstairs when no one else was home. I would feel a presence walk through the room and "hear" suggestions. I sometimes felt a different presence, something scary, but that wouldn't last. Most of the time, I just felt a sense of maternal love. I never considered wanting to have the house freed of its ghosts The house felt like home and the presence was family.

Then active things started happening. I remember having a date and trying to decide what purse to carry. I was upset because I didn't have any that I liked and stated out loud, "I don't know what purse to take. What am I going to do?" All of a sudden, I had this crazy urge. I walked out of my room and opened the storage closet. I put my hand into a barrel and pulled out a purse that matched my outfit beautifully. I had no idea that my grandmother's things were in that barrel. I just followed the urge. I thanked my grandmother for the purse and went out on my date.

Then she began doing things for me. The kindest was when my grandfather was ill. I was going to fix him something to eat but I didn't know what to make. All of a sudden, an idea popped into my mind and that's what I made. It wasn't anything I'd ever made before. When I took it up to grandfather, he said, "How did you know? This is what Betty (my grandmother) would always fix when I was feeling poorly."

I began to feel that grandmother was my guide, but I could only feel her presence when I was in grandfather's house. Then I realized that she was just waiting for grandfather. I think he knew it too. Sometimes he would even call me by her name.

Grandfather had several girlfriends but none would stay for long in the house. These women were old friends from their married life. I often felt that grandmother would tolerate them only so long and then somehow get them to leave. She never did anything bad, but all of them got the drift that grandfather would never remarry.

When I graduated from college, my mother became very uncomfortable with my living arrangements and wanted me to move. I had a good job and made plenty of money to pay for my own place but I had reservations about leaving. I knew that Grandfather could no longer live alone. He had aged a lot in the five years I'd been there and my mother did not understand what she was asking. I knew how hard it would be for me to move out.

Ultimately I decided to make the move to make my parents happy. It was like a divorce. I felt so bad. The only reason I could give Grandfather for moving out was that I wanted to find a mate and get married. He survived my move, but became a permanent fixture at my mother's house. He could not keep up the house and Mother and I would often go over to his house to help.

I was married within six months of moving out. Glen was the only man I knew who could sit in that house and not feel very uncomfortable. I guess he was the only man that both my grandfather and his house would accept! I think my grandmother must have approved, too.

In 1988 I went to the house again about a month after my grandfather died to help with the cleaning and estate sale. I stepped into the house and could immediately feel that grandmother was gone. I even said so to my mother and she just looked at me strangely. She didn't debate the issue and even went so far as to agree that the house did feel different. The house was sold shortly thereafter. I must admit, I still miss my grandmother's ghost, but I am glad that both my grandfather and my grandmother have crossed over together.

As an epilogue, I still hear from both my grandmother and my grandfather from time to time. They have been a great source of strength for me. Now that my Uncle Jack is gone, I have heard from him too. These family members have made so much difference in my life, I have never been afraid of them in death. It also makes me completely unafraid of death itself.

So that's my story. I would appreciate your advice. I spent a lot of years trying to shut down my psychic abilities, but now I would like to develop my gifts with the dead. I just don't know if my problem with the living would be tolerable. Once I open up, I do not know if I could really shut it down again, as you seem to do. Blocking the flood is so hard. It took me years to make my life positive and free from psychic troubles. I just feel that half of me is behind this wall I erected.

I look forward to your reply. I do hope you enjoyed my favorite ghost story. It was a story that crossed several decades and is still a time in my life that I cherish.

Sincerely,

Elizabeth

I spoke to Elizabeth about a year after receiving her letter because I wanted to see how she was doing with her abilities. She told me she had "surrendered" to them and had learned to work with them. She sounded so at peace and no longer had the resistance to opening that psychic door.

If we have psychic abilities and aren't using them, sometimes spirit will bombard us with experiences until we finally say "UNCLE." What I've heard from other people is that all the spirits in their life quieted down once they finally decided to explore their gifts.

You would think that if spirits spend a lot of time trying to get someone to open to their psychic gifts, and they finally do, that the spirits might hang around and communicate with them, but that's not necessarily how it goes. I find that more often than not, once a psychically gifted person decides to open up that door, spirits will often feel that they've accomplished their mission and move on.

Dear Echo,

1) Since I was very young I have been both fascinated and frightened of ghosts. I grew up in a house inhabited by spirits. I remember being about four years old and getting awakened in the middle of the night by a loud hammer-like sound, as if someone were wearing heavy lead shoes, walking up the hallway from the bedrooms toward the kitchen. The pounding stopped and then I heard the sound of dishes crashing to the floor and pots and pans falling out of their assigned places. My whole family marched to the kitchen to see what was happening, but as soon as we turned on the kitchen light the noises STOPPED! Everything was neat and in place. There were no broken dishes or pots and pans on the floor.

My father told everyone "It must be the pipes under the floor. Go back to bed." So we all went back to bed, wanting to trust my father but knowing there must be more to it. It happened at least two more times that I can remember.

2) Once my mother was in the living room with my grand-mother when they heard a heavy hammering. A few minutes later my father came in and my mother asked him why he was making such a racket with the hammer? My father replied, "what are you talking about? I was just walking around the backyard." My father hadn't heard a sound. My grandmother advised my mother to leave! But my mother was about to give birth to my sister and they had nowhere else to go.

3) Before I was old enough to start school, my mother would take a nap every day before my brother came home from school. I would lie on the couch in the living room and listen to a man and woman laughing and talking. I could hear cocktail glasses clinking and the soft sounds of other voices laughing and talking.

It was as if there were a cocktail party going on. This would happen quite frequently.

4) One day, when my brother was sick and unable to leave the house, my parents, my sister and I were sitting in the car waiting to go shopping. We noticed a face staring out of my parents' bedroom window. The hair was dark like my brother's, the face was pale and he seemed to be staring off and not looking at us as we waved good-bye to him. It was a good distance from the car to the bedroom window so none of us had a real close-up look at the face, but we all assumed it was John. Who else would it be? When we arrived home, we asked John why he hadn't waved good-bye to us. He said he never left his bed.

5) By the time I was eleven years old I knew there was a pattern developing. Every night after 11pm, I would hear someone hammering on the roof of the house across the street. At first I wondered who would be working at that time of the night. When the hammering stopped, I would hear someone swinging on the swing in the backyard behind ours. I would listen to the creaking sound, again wondering who would be doing that at this hour. The creaking would stop and I would hear the sound of a very large hammer again, only this time it was under my bed! I prayed to God, afraid to move. I wondered why everyone else wasn't waking up.

6) My grandfather had recently died and one night I called to him for help. After a few minutes I decided to get out of bed and head toward my parent's bedroom, which was right next door to mine. Very cautiously I moved, afraid of what I might find. When I reached the hallway, I saw a very large figure of a man. He was a thick white fog but I could see the outline of every muscle, like in an anatomy book. I must have just stared at him for a few minutes, trying to determine if what I was seeing was real. I was afraid to walk through him or around him to get into my parents' room so I slowly turned around and got back into bed and resumed praying. Thank God that experience never repeated itself, but I always wondered about it.

One day my mother had a group of psychics come over to lead the spirits to the light. They told my mother that a family that used to live in the house was killed in a car crash. They identified a little girl named Mary. That was back in 1968. Since then, I haven't heard another sound but my mother continued to have some troubling experiences. She would complain of cold hands wrapping themselves around her face for example. My father thought it was mid-life crisis.

These days all seems to be quiet on the ghostly front, but still, whenever I visit my parents, I know not to walk down the hallway to their bedroom. I just get a very strong feeling that it's forbidden, which tells me the spirits are still here.

Please give me your opinion and feelings on what you think occurred. Thanking you for your time and energy, I am
Sincerely yours,
Tanya

Dear Tanya:

It sure sounds like your ghosts wanted lots of attention. That was a lot of noise you had to put up with. One thing that's typical about your situation was that your dad never heard or sensed any of the happenings and even chalked it up to your mom being in a mid-life crisis. We've found typically in a haunted house that it's usually the logical, practical, male that doesn't believe in or experience the ghosts whereas the more sensitive, psychic, intuitive women do. It's not always the case, but the majority of cases are like that. An interesting side note to this is that the majority of ghosts I've met are male. Not all of them, but I would say about 80% of the ghosts we've encountered were male in their last life and identify themselves as male.

I'm so glad to hear your mom brought in a psychic to clean up the house. My hunch is that the feeling you still get by your parents' room is just energy left behind from your ghosts. You might want to burn some sage to clear out that old energetic residue. The Solutions chapter will tell you how. I bet the house will feel like new after doing it. Thanks for your letter.

Sincerely,

Echo

This next letter has a little bit of everything in it and certainly brings up a good argument for full disclosure laws when it comes to selling homes that are haunted. After reading about everything this woman and her family went through, I can understand why she's afraid of the dark!

Hi Echo,

I would like to tell you what led me to your book Relax, It's Only a Ghost. *During the summer I went with my husband and kids up to New York to visit my family. While staying at my younger sister's house, we noticed that the house we lived in as kids was up for sale again. This house seemed to go up for sale every couple of years.*

I think the house is a portal to the spirit world, and so does my sister. When we moved in, I was two, and I believe I was about six when we moved out. I am the middle daughter, with a sister a year younger and one a year older. We three girls shared a huge attic bedroom, with one window located at each end. In the center of the room on one wall, was a walk-in closet which opened up into the attic storage area. We never ventured in there. Also on the side of the closet and closest to the stairs was a storage trunk of some type. It was about the size of a coffin. I put my mattress on the trunk and slept there. I can still remember waking one night and thinking that my cat was talking to me (he was lying with me). I heard a voice say, "watch out, he is going to yank your hair" and just then my head was jerked back by my hair.

Another night I woke up and saw a dark hairy creature coming towards me, I sat up and tried to scream, but the "thing" put a hand over my mouth until I finally gave up. Another time we were all down by the fence along the riverbank with some neighborhood kids and we heard a very loud, very horrifying voice yell, "get out of here." As we looked around to see which of us said it, the voice repeated itself. Needless to say we all took off running.

Still another time I told my younger sister to run around the house with me kissing all the door knobs. When my mom told us to stop and asked why we during it, all I could say was: "the little Indian boy told me to."

The only weird memory my older sister has is of waking one night to see an arm extending out of our nightlight, beckoning her to it (it was the type of nightlight popular in the 60s with the little boy praying). My younger sister doesn't remember anything, but my mom told us just a few years ago that she used to suffer night terrors. At night she would wake up screaming with her little

41

fingers blistered, and in the morning they would be back to normal. A few times they actually took her to the hospital but her fingers were always normal by the time they got there. My mom finally had to tell my dad that she thought something was very wrong in the house.

Every night we woke with nightmares and would all end up sleeping downstairs in the living room. During the day the house was very cozy, but at night it was terrifying. There also was a place in the stairway leading up to the bedroom attic that was always very cold. I am sure that I have many more memories of the house that I have blocked.

Anyway, back to the story. So we noticed that the house was for sale again and all of us – my dad, mom, both sisters and brother – got to talking about the house. How it seemed to be shrinking, literally. My husband (who does not believe any of the things I have told him) said we should ask the Realtor if we could see the house. I still dream about the house, and in my dreams I am still not able to gather up the courage to go inside of it. My brother was too young to remember, and my dad worked a lot at night, so he didn't see a lot of the things we did, and my older sister just doesn't want to remember it.

None of us felt we could go into the house, mainly for fear that whatever was in there would come out with us. But when I returned to Florida I couldn't stop thinking about the house. My younger sister and I are very close and we started researching the house. We found out something extremely interesting. It was built in 1938 (or so we believe) and was part of the first settlement along the St. Lawrence River. The house is at an intersection, with a bridge just behind it. The bridge is part of the remains of an Indian stockade, which was used to keep the Indians from entering the town.

When my sister looked on old maps, it appeared that the house sat on what was an old cemetery as well. Historians said they thought the graveyard was located elsewhere, but no one really knows what happened to it. We tried to do research on all the owners prior to us to see if something awful had occurred in the house. The house was sold to a man in 1938 by the woman who owned it. The man lived in it for 2 years and sold it to a couple. The couple lived there for 14 years (the longest anyone has ever lived there) and sold it to another couple, who lived there for 4 years and sold it to my parents. We lived in it for about 4, maybe 5 years, and then sold it. (We heard that the new owners boarded up the attic bedroom area.) Since then the house has been up for sale about every 2 years.

Because of all this my sister decided to join a ghost society and become the spokesperson for that area. She was too scared to go into haunted houses, or to try to do ghost busting, so she decided to start putting together a book on ghost stories for our hometown area. To her surprise, she has been flooded with responses! I will be helping her edit stories and in preparing for that (and because I too am so interested in it), I decided to start checking out as many books as I could find at the library to read how they were done. That is how I came to your book! I just finished it yesterday, and I am just in awe.

A few more stories: On junior prom night I stayed at my boyfriend's house in a nearby town (with his mom there, of course). The room I stayed in used to be his deceased grand-mother's. As I turned off the lights I jumped into bed as quickly as I could (I hate the dark, even now). As I lay there, the foot of the bed went down and I felt a presence sitting there. At first I froze and then I decided not to be afraid. I told myself it must be the grandmother making sure that I stayed in my room and didn't wander down the hall to my boyfriend's during the night.

Another time we (my brother, younger sister and I) were playing in my dad's recording studio. I looked up and saw a man (whom I could literally see through) playing a fiddle. I was horrified, I told my brother and sister to duck down to make sure it wasn't our reflection in the glass – there were soundproof glass booths at each end of the room. They didn't see him. Then we ran into the office and as we got to the door to the house I heard footsteps walking down the hall. Of course when my parents came they didn't see anything. These days I won't even watch movies like "Poltergeist" because I can't stop thinking about the ghosts afterward.

But when my kids were born, I told myself that I would protect them. I remember saying it aloud one night: "I will not be afraid of getting out of our bed in the dark to check on my baby, and you cannot hurt me or my family. I won't let you!"

We built the house we live in now and only a couple of odd things have happened here. One night I was lying in bed with my eyes closed (I sleep very lightly) and I remember hearing my husband say "good night," but when I opened my eyes he wasn't there!

I hope I haven't bored you. I don't have anyone to talk to about my experiences (except my younger sister) and so when I find someone who understands, it all just comes out. Thanks so much, I look forward to reading your other books!

God Bless,

C

Dear C:

No, you certainly didn't bore me. What struck me about all the experiences you had as a little girl is how sad it is that kids are being so frightened by ghosts. You're obviously gifted psychically. It doesn't sound like anyone has ever addressed that. I was so glad to read at the end of your letter that you've put your foot down and told the spirits that you would not let them interfere with your life. That was music to my ears.

I suggest you check out the Clearing Exercise in the Solutions chapter. Being as psychic as you are, you definitely need to be clearing yourself three to four times a day so that you can stay clear and not be affected by everyone else's "stuff" on a psychic level.. Thanks for sharing your experiences.

Sincerely,

Echo

Psychic Abilities

People often write to ask me if I think the psychic experiences they've had are real or imagined. A lot of people worry that their psychic experiences mean they're going crazy or getting into something "evil." Unfortunately there is so much fear and there are so many misconceptions about psychic abilities that people don't know if they should be grateful for having them or get down on their knees and pray for redemption.

I have a new book coming out in January 2003 called *A Gift: Understanding and Developing Your Psychic Abilities* which covers the entire subject of psychics, psychic abilities and how to develop them. If this is an ability you believe you have and are interested in learning more about it and/or developing it, I suggest getting a copy of it. If I've done my job well, it should answer every question you might have and will help you understand and develop your gift. The important thing to remember about psychic development is that it takes time and patience. There are so many things to learn about these gifts and it's important not to be in a hurry.

Here are some letters I've received from writers regarding psychic abilities:

Dear Ms. Bodine:

I finished your book "Relax, it's only a Ghost" this evening. I found it to be quite interesting. I am a retired police officer. I had to retire early due to a motorcycle accident. I'm told I died on the scene but was revived. The reason I bring this up is that I've read that head trauma will or can cause a person to become more receptive psychically. Since the accident, I actually did see a ghost in an 1880s Victorian home after I asked her to appear. Unfortunately, the sight of her scared the hell out of me. Other than that, all I can say is that I get feelings. My question is, how do I learn to channel my psychic ability? If I truly have that ability, that is.

I know you are a very busy person, but any help you could provide in this matter would be greatly appreciated.

Sincerely,

Tony

Dear Tony:

I've also heard that head trauma can open up a person's psychic abilities although I've never personally met a psychic who got their start that way. There was a famous psychic named Peter

Hurkos who was a Dutch house painter. He fell from his ladder one day and when he came out of his coma (I hope I'm remembering this accurately) he had strong psychic abilities and it changed his life forever.

As strange as this sounds, I frequently get my skull bones adjusted by my chiropractor (it's called cranio-sacral work) and it helps to keep my psychic channel opened up so I can *kind of* understand how this could happen.

I had to laugh when I read your comment about the ghost. So often when people want to see a ghost really badly and it finally happens, it does scare the heck out of them. That's what happened to me!

Sincerely,

Echo

Hi Echo,

I'm a police officer and many strange things happen in my home – things move around, the water turns on by itself, the toilet flushes, and my dog and cat react to invisible stuff. It's all pretty bizarre. My wife and I have become pretty used to it. We've been in the house for 3 years and all of the activity seems to center around one room. Whenever something happens I write it down just to keep track and I now have about nine pages of ghostly incidents.

When ghosts are photographed sometimes they show up as orbs [circles] and sometimes they show up foggy. Do you ever see them in the orb shape or is that just how the camera picks up the energy? I'm very "sensitive," I get very uncomfortable when there are bad vibes, for example when people are angry at one another. Is it possible to train myself to become more psychic?

Can someone learn to see ghosts the way that you do?

I hope my questions aren't too silly. Thank you for your time. Keep up the great work,

Marty

Dear Marty:

First of all, I can't imagine how tough it would be to have psychic abilities and be a cop! I get a third eye headache just thinking about it.

To answer your question regarding pictures of ghosts, I've seen them both ways. Orbs and foggy or smoky images. There've been a few times on ghostbusting jobs when I've taken pictures of the fully formed spirits I saw, but when the pictures came back there were orbs (energy circles) in the photo, some large, some small. I don't have a scientific explanation for why this happens, I just know it does.

Your last question is whether or not people can learn to see ghosts. The answer is yes. Seeing ghosts is called clairvoyance, and you can train yourself to become clairvoyant. It involves training your third eye, which is located in the middle of your forehead, to see ghosts and pick up psychic information in the form of visions and images. There are some wonderful books on the market that can help you develop your psychic abilities. See the Recommended Book List at the end of the book. Also, ask God to send you a teacher so that you don't have to do this all by yourself.

I strongly suggest getting in the habit of asking God to put a purple cloak of protection around you whenever you leave the house and especially when you go to work. You mentioned feeling bad vibes when people are angry at one another which indicates to me that you have clairsentience, which is the gift of sensing. As a policeman, I can only imagine the kind of vibes you're around all day, so I want you to get in the habit of also doing the Clearing Exercise in the Solutions chapter whenever you feel "off" mentally or psychically.

Sincerely

Echo

To Dearest Echo

My name is Jon. I live in London and I am 23 years old. I would just like to say how glad I was to read your book. I could not put it down. Since I was a young boy my life has been governed by ghosts and spirits. I have had some awful times and I also have slight e.s.p. It has not been easy. I have lost a lot of my feelings. My mum died 5 years ago and since then I fed a lot of my grief by drinking and doing drugs. Now I have stopped and I want to channel my gift right but I may need to get over my mum first. Thank you very much for that book. It was a fresh breath of sunshine to read it.

Jon

Hello Jon:

First of all, I'm sorry about the loss of your mom. I can only imagine how tough that is.

Before you get into your psychic development, I suggest doing whatever you can to get on your spiritual path. It's really important to have a good spiritual foundation in your life if you want to develop psychically. Are you attending AA or a similar 12 Step program? The meetings and especially the Twelve Steps are an excellent source for growing spiritually. I highly recommend them.

I also want you to get a copy of my book, *A Still Small Voice:
A Psychic's Guide to Awakening Intuition* (New World Library).
Between working the Twelve Steps and living by your intuition,
you couldn't get a stronger spiritual foundation, which in turn will
make your psychic development easier. You'll know intuitively
when the time is right to start developing your psychic gifts. I wish
you the best of success in your sobriety and your new life. I would
imagine your mom is very proud of you.
God Bless,
Echo

Dear Echo,

*I recently bought and read your new book Relax, It's Only a
Ghost and I thought it was awesome. Such a great book, I'm
about to read it again. I'm not a psychic or healer nor do I claim
to be, but at times I sense strange things. I hear things that aren't
there and for some reason I feel very uneasy in some people's
homes and very comfortable in others.*

*One day when I was about 12, I was in my church, playing
on the piano, and I saw a floating image pass by the window.
I knew for some reason that it was my dead grandfather.*

*A few years later, after my daddy's grandmother had passed
on, we went to stay with his grandfather for the night and I felt the
most nauseating, horrible feeling all night. I was so scared. I
heard wailing sounds and gnashing sounds, almost evil. I couldn't
wait to leave.*

*A few years after that my 16-year-old cousin came by to see
me and for some reason I cried when he left. I knew I wouldn't
see him again and he seemed to know too. Two days later he
was killed in a car wreck.*

I was awake lying in bed about a month ago and could have sworn I heard male voices chanting together saying, "freedom, freedom, freedom." It scared the daylights out of me. Sometimes I hear clanking and one night the pans in my sink just banged rather loudly. It's scary.

About five years ago a little girl was raped and murdered about a quarter-mile down the road. I didn't even live here at the time – there wasn't even a house here then – and I've often wondered whether she visits here.

I have a toddler little girl and her toys sometimes come on by themselves while she's sitting in my lap. I have also caught her playing "peek-a-boo" with no one there and just laughing. She's only a year old so she can't tell me if she is seeing anyone.

Could you please help me? You know, just some peace of mind and maybe an answer? I would really appreciate it, and just so you know, none of this is made up and it's not intended as a prank. I'm sure you get plenty of those. Thank you ever so much.

Sincerely,

CC

Dear CC:

The experiences you shared sound very hard to go through and I think it's really unfortunate you haven't had someone around to help you understand what you're going through.

It definitely sounds like you've got clairaudience, which is the gift of hearing spirit. That's how you were able to hear those spirit voices chanting "freedom" and how you heard the clanking sounds of the pans. *Knowing* the spirit at the church was your grandfather and *knowing* you were never going to see your cousin again, was that inner *knowing* we get from our intuition.

It's tough to say who your daughter is playing peek-a-boo with. The fact that she doesn't react negatively tells me this is not a negative spirit messing with her. It could be the murdered little girl looking for someone to play with or it could simply be a deceased relative or her guardian angel. It's not unusual for children to see spirits and we can tell by their reaction if the presence is positive or negative. In this case, it certainly sounds like she's doing fine with whomever it is.

I would suggest doing the Clearing Exercise outlined in the Solutions chapter. It will help you feel more grounded with your psychic abilities. I also suggest checking out the Recommended Book List at the end of the book and ask your intuition to guide you to the right books for you.

God Bless,

Echo

Dear Echo Bodine,

I am praying that you might be able to help me, or more directly, my boyfriend. He has seen ghosts and spirits since he was very young but lately feels as if he is going crazy. He cannot control it in any way. He sees flashes of visions and he sees people but cannot make sense of it most of the time. I tell him to consider it a gift, for he has, on several occasions, had visions or feelings that have kept us out of danger and harm's way. He says he is sick of all the death and pain he sees and feels like he is losing his mind.

To tell you a little about him, he has seen things since he was about four years old. He didn't say anything to anyone for years because he was afraid that he would be thought of as insane. He now sees them (ghosts and spirits) on a regular basis. He can drive by a house and tell if there are ghosts or spirits in it and has amazed quite a few of his customers (he's a general contractor) when he goes into a house he is to do work on and can tell its owners about the past events that have happened there – if there have been deaths or other occurrences.

I don't mean to sound corny, but the mobile home park where we live, and where he has lived his whole life, was at one time an Indian war field or burial ground of some sort. Arrowheads can be found all over the property. For years my boyfriend has been seeing the bottom half of an Indian man sticking out of his mom's front yard, and he and his older son both have seen what they call the "hatchet man" in our front and side yard and the woods behind our house. It is, as they have both described separately, a man dressed in leather pants, with long hair and paint, holding what looks like a tomahawk or small hatchet.

His older son has seen ghosts and spirits for about seven years. The first was his dead grandfather, whom he had never met but could describe perfectly. His younger son hears voices calling him, as if trying to get him to go somewhere. He also sees what he describes as a big black horse with huge white teeth in his bedroom closet. I thought at first it was his version of a closet monster, but my boyfriend has seen it also. He says it is bad. He doesn't know how or why, he says he just knows it is something (definitely not a horse) trying to entice his son. He tells him to just stay away from it.

I have never actually seen these things, but I have heard them and felt their presence. Sometimes I can hear them walking down the hallway. Even the cats we used to have would sometimes get only halfway down the hall, stop, and turn back toward the kitchen again, hissing and spitting.

Our house has affectionately become known as Spook Central, with the back hallway to the bedrooms as Grand Central Station. The ghosts and/or spirits seem to originate or manifest at the step down from the kitchen to the back hallway. Every once in a while one will come up front and out the front door, but most move the other way. They go past the younger son's bedroom. They usually go past our bedroom. Sometimes they will walk in and stand next to him while he's in bed. They always head for the older son's room. Ever since he can remember, my boyfriend has seen a porthole at the end of that room. He describes it as a black hole, total darkness. These ghosts/spirits often try to get him to enter the porthole, which, he says, is sometimes very difficult for him to ignore.

What scares me most, for his sake, is that sometimes he leaves his body while he is sleeping. I can actually sense that he is "not here." His body physically changes. His breathing is almost non-existent, and he looks as if he is deflated. When asked about it he'll say, "oh, I was visiting."

He leaves his body and can see himself sleeping, and he'll sometimes moves from room to room to check on his sons. He has even been called out of the house once. He says he was walking through a darkened field, pitch black, and all he could see was a basement window. There was a young boy at the window pleading to be let out. He said that as nice as the boy looked, something didn't seem right, and he told the little boy he could not let him out. As he told him this, the boy turned into something he wouldn't describe as anything more than a monster beast that became angry and beat at the window trying to break free. He returned to his body and as he woke, even he was scared by what had happened.

I think that he sees more than he lets on. When I ask him about it though he just says there is too much death and sickness and he doesn't know what to do.

Is there some way he can control these visions or help these souls that he sees? Please, I pray that you can give me some kind of advice or guidance to help him figure out how to deal with his ability, or curse, as he puts it. He would love to pursue more information on this but I am his book reader. He has a learning disability that makes reading very difficult. I do what I can to try to help him, and I felt that if anyone could help it would be you. I would greatly appreciate any help or recommendation you could give. There are so many souls and so much unhappiness involved that I feel like I'm losing the battle of holding things together and losing him in the process.

With Much Hope,

HC

Dear HC:

My heart certainly goes out to you and your boyfriend. He's obviously developed and used his gifts in former lives, which is why his abilities are so strong without any formal training. I'm sorry to hear he can't shut it off, but I assure you, he can learn how.

I want you both to know that he is stronger than any of these entities he's seeing and that with a strong, persuasive voice, he could get them to move on to the other side.

As far as being afraid of the port hole he sees in the bedroom, if he ever feels ready to venture into it, he'll see it's simply an opening to the astral plane. It's nothing that will hurt him and his soul is very aware of what it is, which is probably why he doesn't want to go there. There's no reason to.

The theme that runs through my mind as I read your letter is that you are giving these experiences way too much power. You need to read up on Astral Projection. I recommend Robert Monroe's book, *Journeys Out of the Body*. I cover the subject to a small degree in Chapter 5 but since he's so proficient at it, I would suggest getting a book that covers all aspects of it. My sense is that once you both have more knowledge about ghosts, astral projection, and life after death, you will feel less powerless to do anything. Knowledge is power and I want you both to gain as much knowledge as you can because my guess is, his abilities aren't going to go away. They'll just continue to get stronger over time.

I have a couple more suggestions: Try to find the gem or gift in each experience. My sense is that the gem is bringing comfort either to the living or the dead, whichever he happens to be dealing with.

My other suggestion is to get a copy of my book *Echoes of the Soul*. This book is all about the soul's perspective of life, death and life after death. Many people have told me this book has brought them peace of mind regarding death, and I think it will help both of you as well. I think it's also important to pass on the information to his sons, since it sounds like they've inherited his abilities. Thanks for writing. I wish you all the very best on your journey.

Sincerely,

Echo

Dear Echo,

I wanted to tell you about a strange experience I had when I first asked for help in finding your book.

As soon as I asked for help finding your book at Barnes & Noble, I got a pressure between my ears that felt like the rush of blood from altitude pressure. It hung onto me until I grabbed both books that were there. I thought it was just strange and meant nothing, but I wondered. Then a few days later I went shopping with a friend and I told her about the strange experience. As I said your name, it happened again. Then every time I said your name it happened again!

I think I was being told that you would touch my life. You already have, so I do not know why it is still going on. I have never felt this feeling before except when I was driving though low and high altitudes, but this was stronger. So much that my brain began to buzz. I hope I'm not ill or something!

Just wanted to share that with you.

Love and peace

R

Dear R:

You have no idea how interesting your email is – the experiences you had and the timing of it.

I was going through a psychic shift over the course of about ten days, and it happened to be right at the time you emailed me. My psychic eye, located in the middle of my forehead, was opening up to a higher level and usually when that happens I go through physical symptoms that feel exactly like the ones you described in the email. I've been doing alot of cranio-sacral work with my chiropractor (literally adjusting the bones in my skull) and taking herbs to help relieve that pressure that you spoke of. It amazes me that you could feel that pressure simply by thinking of me or my books. You undoubtedly have psychic abilities.

If this ever happens again, with me or anyone else for that matter, try the Clearing Exercise, which you'll find in the Solutions chapter. That will help you to stay clear of other people's energy.

Thanks so much for writing.

God Bless

Echo Bodine

Dear Echo,

My name is JJ and I live in Minnesota. I am writing to say that I heard you last week on the KQ92 morning show with Tom Barnard and the Gang. I went directly to Barnes and Noble and bought your book Relax, It's Only a Ghost. I read the whole book in a couple of hours. I found it to be very interesting and helpful in my own development. I am sure you hear this all the time but I once saw a ghost and on a different occasion I felt a presence. The ghost I saw consisted only of a head wearing a straw hat. I was never afraid of this ghost. He actually seemed as intrigued by me as I was by him. I have never encountered another ghost. Is this normal or common?

Sincerely,

JJ

Dear JJ:

Your experience is more normal than you might think. Lots of times people see only a portion of a ghost. The reason for this is simple. Spirits are made of energy and it's not easy for them to materialize. That's why we read or hear stories of floating heads or ghosts without legs or feet. It doesn't mean they're not all there, it just means this is all they're able to manifest and all we're able to see.

Your letter reminded me of an odd experience my sister Nikki and I had back in 1966. I was 18, my sister was 12. Her bedroom was across the hall from mine. At about 3 one morning, I sat straight up in my bed. I noticed I hadn't been sleeping in the middle of the bed like I usually did, I'd been sleeping all the way over to the left. The right side of the bed was very smooth with the covers turned down, which I found very odd. It looked like it had been prepared for someone else.

I looked across the hall at my sister's room and *knew* something was about to happen. I didn't move a muscle. I just sat there silently when suddenly my sister came flying into my room. She dove into my bed. Neither of us said a word. I wanted to talk but I couldn't. We just laid down and I held her hand and we went to sleep.

The next morning she must have woken up before I did and gone back to her room because I didn't remember anything until we were at breakfast. My sister had never been affected by all the spirit activity that went on in our house. In fact she thought we were all a little crazy. So as I sat there remembering what had taken place during the night, I couldn't help wondering if I'd dreamed it.

She was the one to bring it up. She asked me if I remembered her coming into my room in the middle of the night. She said she had seen half of a male figure standing at the side of her bed and that she tried to yell out, but nothing came out of her mouth. That's when she bolted out of bed and ran into my room. We talked about how weird it was that neither of us said a word and that the bed had been made up as if it was waiting for her. It gave us the willies just talking about it, so we chalked it up to another one of *those* experiences and never mentioned it again.

Your other comment about your ghost appearing only once is also common. I think once they know that we know they're there, appearing to us becomes less important. They've gotten our attention and that's what matters. Thanks for your letter JJ.

Sincerely,

Echo

Dear Echo,

My name is MM. My fiance and I and our two kids bought a new house two years ago and we believe we have a ghost or two. It started when we first bought the house and I was pregnant with our second child. We hadn't moved in yet but were doing some work in the garage when I just happened to glance into the house from the kitchen door. I saw something white float into the baby's nursery. I freaked out and got into the car and told my fiance that I did not want to work on the house anymore that night! I explained what I had seen and we left.

After we moved in, more weird stuff happened. One night we went to our bowling league and when we came home all our kitchen cabinet doors were open. Sometimes we can be in the living room and our kids be in bed and our kitchen door will open and slam by itself. We have even found ourselves talking to the ghost. We thought we were talking to each other but we weren't! Once I was in the bathroom and thought my fiance was talking to me and said, "hold on," and when I came out and asked what he wanted he said, "I didn't say anything. I was in here in the living room the whole time!" Also, once when we *were working on the house before we moved in I was outside and felt someone looking at me from the bedroom window.*

So I'm pretty sure we have a ghost or two here. My little sister and I got on her [Ouija] board and asked her spirit friend if we had one in our house and he said we have 2, a man and a woman. He told us that the woman watches over the baby but he did not say much about the man. I am not sure how much you charge to make a home visit but if you could let me know, we would save up for you to come and put our minds to ease. Thank you for your time.

Dear MM:

Assuming that you received accurate information from the Ouija Board (and I have my doubts), a thought that occurred to me while reading your letter is that possibly the man is the original builder of the house because it sounds like the ghost is agitated about the changes you're making.

My brother Michael and I were called to a house in St. Paul several years ago. There had been no unusual activity until the new homeowners decided to add a room onto the house and then all hell seemed to break loose. Banging on the walls, the sounds of footsteps, tools being moved, a cold chill moving through people.

I remember this job in particular because usually when we ask a ghost for its name, it will give us a first name, but this ghost told us his name was Mr. Peterson. He explained that he was the original owner and builder of the home and had to protect it from all the changes the new owners wanted to make. That's why he was making all this noise and moving their tools. We've found similar situations in other homes that are being remodeled by new owners.

The way we handled the ghostbusting job with Mr. Peterson was that we told him he could build an even better home in Heaven (which he could) and that it was important that he let go of this house and go over to the other side. We had to repeat this to him several times because he didn't believe it was possible, but we convinced him that in Heaven anything's possible. He did move on and the people had no more problems renovating their home.

I suggest you try this with your ghosts.

Sincerely,

Echo

Chapter Four

When Loved Ones Come Back to Visit

*P*eople often ask me how they can tell if the odd happenings in their homes are signs from deceased loved ones that they're visiting or if they actually have a ghost. It's actually easy to tell: just notice how you feel when they're around. If you feel comforted and at ease, you're in the presence of a loved one; if you feel scared or tense, your visitor is a ghost.

As you know by now, the house I grew up in was filled with ghostly presences, but I could always tell when it was my deceased grandpa visiting because I would feel comforted by his presence. I never felt comforted when a ghost was around, but when grandpa came he'd project the smell of vanilla ice cream or green tea and I'd know it was him. I felt protected by him. Grandpa would sometimes sit on my bed and I would always feel calm. When an earthbound spirit would sit on my bed, it felt cold and frightening and I'd usually dive under the covers.

In this first letter, we see the same dynamic. This young woman's deceased grandfather came and comforted her when she was contemplating suicide, but when she and her sister came face to face with a ghost, they were very frightened. Always check how you feel around the spirit presence and you'll know whether you're dealing with a ghost or a friend.

Dear Echo,

    I have always felt that I had sensitivity to spirits. Several times in my life I've been visited by deceased family members. It was great how you talked about saying the Lord's prayer to ease the fear, because that was always the tool I used. My grandfather has spoken to me, but I've never talked back. I'm still pretty fearful. Is it possible he is a guide of some sort or guardian angel? When I was very depressed and contemplated suicide, he told me to hang on.

    Also, if I sit in a particular chair or touch a certain item I get intense feelings.

    I don't want to take up too much of your time, I just felt compelled to write. Your book really gave me a thirst to delve further into the paranormal world. Now more than ever I would love to get a reading. Do you have any recommendations on how to choose the right person?

    I also wanted to share my only real ghost story. This happened many years ago when I was 6 or 7 and my older sister was nine. We had come home from a picnic and my sister and I were anxious to give our parents some cards that we had made for them. We had hidden the cards in the basement. My sister didn't want to go down there, so she said she would turn on the light but I had to get the cards, which were at the far end of the basement. I remember feeling scared for the first time. When my sister tried to turn the light on she got a horrible shock. I ran past her up the stairs, scared out of my mind.

We never talked about the incident until about 10 years later. The whole family was sitting around the table talking about that night when I mentioned that I had seen a man dressed in black standing over my sister as I ran up the stairs. I could see my sister getting paler and paler. It turns out she had seen the same man! We love to tell this story, but after reading your book I have a desire to see if I can find out more about the house and its history.

Dear Writer:

Yes, it is possible that your grandfather is helping to guide you. Throughout my life I've often received little one liners of advice from a male voice. I'm pretty sure it's my grandpa.

It's important that we not confuse deceased loved ones and spirit guides. We all have spirit guides whose purpose is to give us guidance and help us (our soul) stay on track, according to our life plan. Our deceased loved ones can also be guides but it's been my experience that they do not take the place of our spirit guides. It may be too difficult for our deceased loved ones to detach themselves emotionally from what we need to go through and they aren't able to be objective. That's why the Elders on the other side won't allow them to act as guides for family members here on Earth.

About psychic readings, I always recommend that people go to someone they've heard good things about. Don't just go to someone you find in a newspaper. Just as in any profession, there are quacks out there, so ask around for a good referral. You might trying asking your friends or co-workers if they can recommend a reputable psychic.

Be sure to ask what kind of readings the person does. Many psychics specialize in a certain area, such as past lives, future predictions, communicating with the deceased, reading your soul's life plan, and some do general readings. It's important for you to know what you want so that you can go to the psychic who will be able to get that for you. If you can't find a reputable psychic, I would suggest going to my website echobodine.com and look under Consultations/Referrals. I keep an updated referral list of excellent psychics who all work over the phone as well as in person.

One last thought. I just want to caution you to ask your intuition to guide you when picking out books to read. There are lots of books out there. Some are wonderful, some aren't so wonderful. When you're drawn to a book, hold it in your hand and *feel* if it *feels intuitively* right that you should read that book. If you *feel* a desire to read it, then get it. If you're buying it because the cover is pretty, that's not necessarily the book for you. Your inner voice will guide you every step of the way, not only on what books to read, but also which lectures to attend, which psychics to go to, what speakers to trust. You just have to be willing to take the time to listen to it.

Regarding your ghost story, I'm so glad you and your sister had the experience together so that you could validate for each other that it really did happen.

Sincerely,

Echo

Here is another letter from a reader who had two completely different encounters with the spirit world – one with ghosts and the other with a deceased family member. Because her ghosts were just young girls, she wasn't afraid, but as you'll see her visits with her deceased dad had a whole different quality. He actually ended up becoming a guardian spirit for her family.

Dear Ms. Bodine,

I have always been very interested in spirits, ghosts, reincarnation and all that goes along with the supernatural and the things we don't know about our vast universe. I do have a couple of stories to share with you.

Back in 1980, in the summer, my family and I went to a cottage up north near a lake. We'd been to this cottage before. I was 27 years old and 6 months pregnant with my second child. I think it was the day before we had to leave for home that I had my experience with two young female spirits.

To get to the only bathroom in the cottage, you had to go through my bedroom, so I could hear anyone coming and going (I am a very light sleeper). Anyway, sometime after midnight I thought I heard the back door slam shut. (My mother and I made sure it was locked before we went to bed.) All of a sudden I heard footsteps shuffling through my bedroom to the bathroom, I know this was not a mortal thing going on here. I think my heart stopped beating for a while.

I tried so hard to turn (I was facing the wall) to see what these ghosts or spirits looked like and what they wanted. I knew they were young girls because they giggled a lot as they passed through the room. Finally, I turned, and in front of me in the doorway stood two very whitish and fuzzy looking young girls – they wore dresses, but no shoes or socks. I could not see their faces clearly. I just lay there in bed and didn't know what to do or say. They suddenly disappeared.

I started to cry a little, I guess because I felt so privileged that they let me see them. And also because I felt very sad that they may have died at a young age. I believe they may have been twins. All of a sudden, I heard horse hooves pounding up the dirt driveway. And the girls were still giggling aloud.

The next morning I told my mother the story and she said she thought she'd heard the back door slam after we went to bed and it was open when she got up in the morning! She is the only believer I have in the family. I wish I could have communicated with them. I have no idea why they came there or why they were still earthbound.

My next story is about my father. We were close and I loved him deeply. He died in August of 1997 of heart disease and kidney failure. I held his hand when he passed and told him I was sorry for any bad things I did and asked his forgiveness. Also that I loved him and would miss him so much. I asked him to be my daughter's and the rest of the family's guardian angel and to watch over all of us.

About a month after he died he came to me in a vision when I was sleeping. We were in the family station wagon (I think it was a '65 Comet). I was driving and my brothers and sisters were there and he was sitting in the way back seat. He looked about 40 years old – very healthy and slim – he had on the old black glasses that he'd worn in his younger days. Telepathically, with his very nice smile, he told me that he was very happy and everything was okay. He told me not to worry. I told no one of this vision.

The next time he came to me, I was having some problems with my youngest daughter. He told me (telepathically of course) that I must resolve the problem or things would get much worse, so I did and everything is okay now.

The third time was when my mom was having problems with her new garage door and a nosy neighbor. (This man has been *harassing her and all of us girls forever.) Anyway, my dad appeared and told me that the door would be fixed, not to worry. He also wanted me to tell my mom not to let "Ken" into the house at anytime. He obviously knows that Ken's intentions are not good and that it bothers my mother badly. Sometimes she won't even go outside in case he comes over.*

I told my mom about these visions and she started crying. I think she believes in me and she's happy my father still takes care of us. I hope he will continue to visit me throughout my life — I really need him sometimes. Thank you so much for reading this story of mine.

Sincerely,

Janet

Dear Janet:

From the stories you shared about your dad, I'm quite confident he'll continue to give you guidance. It sounds important to him that you know he's watching over you and your family. Your description of him looking healthy and slim like he did when he was in his forties is an accurate account of the transformation we all go through after death when we let go of the earth plane and begin a new life on the other side.

The story about the two young girl spirits brings up a question that I've had when we've encountered children spirits and you might be wondering the same thing. Why doesn't someone from the other side come and take them home?

My sense is that most of the time there is someone from the other side that comes and takes these young souls home but that's not always the case as evidenced by the many children spirits we've run into.

I remember one ghostbusting job we went on where there was a little boy earthbound spirit who appeared to be about five years old living inside the bedroom closet. He said that his family lived down the street and he stayed here rather than go on to heaven so that he could see his mommy everyday. A little girl spirit also lived in that closet but she let me know right away that she was from the other side and was only here to keep the boy company! This house also had a teenage ghost. When we managed to convince him to move on to the other side, we asked that he please take the other children with him, which he did.

I told a story in *Relax, It's Only a Ghost* about a group of six children spirits who had lived and died together in an orphanage in Minneapolis. When I asked them why they didn't move on, they said that they wanted to stay here and play. Even though the orphanage had burned down, they chose a home close by because the area was familiar to them and they wanted to stay there rather than go somewhere they weren't familiar with!

Another reason children spirits remain earthbound is if a grieving family member begs them to stay here. I was a guest on a television show in Seattle called *Northwest Afternoon*. People in the audience and viewers called in and asked questions about ghosts and life after death. One woman called to say that she had lost a child and was praying to this child everyday to help her get through life! Unfortunately this wasn't the first time I had heard something like this. Our grief can hold some of these spirits to the earth plane, which isn't good for anyone. The best thing we can do when we lose someone to death is to release them and tell them to go to the light. To encourage someone to remain earthbound is encouraging them to stay stuck, and that's never good for anyone.

Many people think the term poltergeist (a ghost supposed to be responsible for mysterious noisy disturbances) means a child spirit that is causing damage but that's not the true definition nor do children spirits usually cause damage. They tend to do child-like things, such as playing with toys, singing songs, or hanging out with the children in the house they're "haunting," but they never seem to cause any real problems.

Sometimes all these kids need is a little reassurance and some guidance crossing over. Thanks for sharing your stories.

Sincerely,

Echo

Chapter Five

Possession and Astral Projection

I get lots of letters about possession. Some of you who have never had to deal with this probably think this is a topic better suited for the Jerry Springer show but the truth is, possession really does occur and it's important to understand what it's all about.

Spirit possession goes on more than you might think. Trouble is, most of us got our ideas about possession from the movie *The Exorcist*. We hear the word and think of someone who vomits green pea soup while her head spins, but that's not how it goes at all. It's been my experience that the spirit possessing a person usually wants to draw as little attention to itself as possible.

I've had a couple of direct experiences with possession that I'd like to share with you. When I was in my early twenties, I was a practicing alcoholic. My psychic development teacher once explained to us that the haze in bars isn't all cigarette smoke. She said that some of it is actually the spirit of alcohol or drug-addicted earthbound souls looking for a body to enter so that they can experience their high again. At the time I didn't want to believe her and told myself that she was saying these things so I wouldn't drink. But then I had a couple of experiences that convinced me she was right. One time I went out and drank way too much and the next morning I saw someone else's eyes looking back at me from the mirror! The eyes give it away every time. It was gross, to say the least. Fortunately for me, my teacher taught me that to get rid of these leeches, I simply needed to look them straight in the eye (in the mirror) and demand they get them out of me NOW. She said to do this as soon as I discovered there was someone else inside me and it worked very well.

A few years later, I experienced possession of a different sort. I was teaching a psychic development class and I wanted to show my students what it was like to *channel* information from a spirit. I opened myself up psychically and asked for an evolved spirit to enter my body and *channel* a message to my class. Back in the 60s and 70s, this was called being in a trance, today it's called channeling. I saw a male spirit coming towards me and I had a good feeling about him. He entered my body and spoke through me, answering whatever questions my class asked. When we were done, I saw him step outside my body and go back into the light. About ten minutes later, I got a right side "headache." The whole right side of my body felt off and I couldn't figure out what was wrong with me. For the next two days, the headache continued and I felt very depressed. I felt out of sync with everything but I couldn't put my finger on what it was.

I called a good friend of mine who is a psychic and asked her if I could pay her a visit. As soon as I walked through her front door she asked me if I had recently done some trance work. She said she could see a female spirit standing half in my body and half out, on the right side. As soon as she pointed this out, I remembered that a couple of my students had also said they'd seen a female spirit standing behind me on the right side. They both said she disappeared after the male spirit left me. She had obviously popped into my body as soon as he exited. I didn't notice because I was so focused on him leaving.

My friend sternly told the female spirit to leave my body. She asked her spirit guides to take the spirit home to the other side, and instantly the headache stopped and I felt like my old self.

The problem with movies and religion is that they give the impression that possession is something all powerful and mystical and that only a few gifted priests can get rid of the spirits, but that's not true. The spirits that inhabit our bodies are tortured souls but they're not all that powerful. If you think you're being possessed, you need to demand that the spirit leave you and ask God to take the spirit home. People don't believe they have the power to make something like this happen, so they remain victims and the vicious cycle of possession continues. The point is, we *do* have the power. We just have to use it, and ask for God's help.

Where it can get complicated is if more than one entity is inhabiting a person. There can be several at a time and the way to tell is if the person seems to have different personalities coming and going. If that's what you're dealing with, you do need to call in a trained clergyperson, shaman or healer. They can get these entities out of you and on to the other side. Once again, the key is that the possessed person has to *want* this condition to change.

A guy I went to barber school with approached me cautiously one day and asked if I knew how to help someone who was possessed. He explained that four different entities would take turns living in his body. The guy did seem to have a couple of different personalities but it had never occurred to me that he might be possessed. I told him that I'd be glad to help out in any way I could.

My intention was to do a healing on him and ask Jesus to come and remove the entities and take them home. I had done this with a couple of clients and it was very effective, so I was confident we could get them out of there. We set a time to do it but when the day arrived, he wouldn't speak to me or look me in the eyes all day. He took off as soon as school was over and for the rest of the semester he avoided me. He obviously wasn't ready for change.

As I've already said, it's important for the possessed person to want their situation healed or they'll just attract new spirits to them when the old ones are removed.

Here are two letters from readers who actually saw a spirit trying to take someone over:

Dear Echo,

I need to ask you about an experience I had a couple of months ago.

My husband is an alcoholic. He's not mean or abusive. He has enough to drink each day so that he can, in his words, "get a good night's sleep." One night we were at a restaurant and, just after the waitress served him his first drink, I saw a male spirit appear out of nowhere and go into my husband's body. I sat there quite stunned. I didn't know what to say or do. I watched my husband's mannerisms and paid close attention to his eyes, because I wanted to understand what was going on. I must say, he did seem like a different man.

He was much more animated than my husband normally is but he also had a heavy "vibe." I can't quite describe what I mean, but he definitely was different than my husband. I found myself wanting to get away from him and yet, at the same time, wondered if I was making the whole thing up.

My husband definitely drank more than usual that night and I drove us home. He fixed another drink as soon as we walked in the door and eventually passed out in his chair, which isn't like my husband at all. Right after he passed out, as clearly as I saw this spirit enter my husband, I saw him step out of his body. Then he left our house, as if in a hurry.

This whole experience was pretty upsetting and I haven't shared it with anyone. Do you think I made the whole thing up? Any advice would be greatly appreciated. By the way, as far as I know, this has only happened once. Do you think it's happening without my knowledge? What should I do if it occurs again?

Thanks for your help.

Lee M.

Dear Lee:

I've been through a similar situation where I saw a spirit enter a friend of mine who was a drug addict, so I know exactly what you're talking about. I don't believe for a second that you imagined it. This is an excellent example of how possession can occur. The good news is that the spirit left your husband without having to do anything.

If someone has a noticeable personality change and their eyes look like someone else's, you know they're being possessed with someone else's soul. That's all there is to it. In fact, it's been my experience, when exorcising a soul out of a possessed person, that the spirit will avoid looking at anyone because it knows that the eyes are a dead giveaway. Any time you suspect that your husband may be possessed by a spirit, call on your guardian angels, God, Jesus or whoever you call your Higher Power, and ask them to please come and take the spirit home to the other side. Since your husband is an alcoholic and this kind of situation isn't uncommon, I'd suggest that you ask your husband's spirit guides to watch over his body and not let anyone else's soul come in.

Sincerely,

Echo

Where things can get tricky is that troubled spirits go for people who were similar to them when they were living: drug addicts, alcoholics, people who suffer from depression or people who committed suicide. These people are so down they often don't care what happens to their body, and don't care if someone else takes over their life. It's really hard to stand by and watch when something like this happens, but until the person wants to be free of the possessing spirit, there's not a lot you can do other than pray that they become aware that they have a problem followed by a solution.

Here's another letter dealing with possession:

Hi, I feel uncomfortable even writing this email. Last year my daughter remarried a man whose father passed away 21 years ago when he was piloting his private plane. Apparently his father's spirit, or I should say ghost, has been haunting him on and off for years. He didn't mention this to my daughter until after she had her first encounter with the ghost months ago.

My daughter has a little boy from a previous marriage and 3 stepchildren from this marriage. I never believed in ghosts but the two youngest children seem to see this ghost and he talks to my daughter, touches her and is getting downright out of hand. She is very afraid and it is affecting my little grandson greatly. He senses his presence and has nightmares and such. I think that he even enters my new son-in-law from time to time because of some strange things that have happened. He not only haunts the house where they live but also goes in the car with them. What should they do to get rid of this spirit? I hope that you can help.

Thank you.

S

Dear S:

My guess is that the father won't go on to the other side on his own if he's been hanging around for twenty-one years. If his son allows this to go on, I'd say there's obviously some pretty unhealthy boundary issues going on between father and son. I must say, I'm surprised to hear that the ghost gets in the car with them. They usually choose to stay around the home. You definitely need to call on the Squadron (see Solutions chapter) and ask them to take this man home.

Sincerely,

Echo

This next letter is not about possession, but points out the Universal principle which is *like attracts like.*

Dear Echo Bodine,

Hi, I am 39 years old and a married mother of three. In a previous marriage I lived with a ghost for two years. Just quickly I would like to run by some of the things that this ghost enjoyed.

We had reason to believe that the ghost was a female who in life owned a huge furniture store and was an alcoholic. Since my first husband was also an alcoholic we all got along very well. You could often hear her high heels running up the stairs and clicking along the floor above. Once I heard something (it sounded like glass) crash to the floor. The clicking of the heels stopped and then she continued walking in the counterclockwise circle that she favored. When I went up later to see what had happened there was nothing out of place, nothing broken.

Another time I was lying in bed with my husband early in the morning and I heard the cowbells on the door jingle and the familiar heels coming up the stairs. (The door was locked and no one else had the key.) I then heard the refrigerator door open and the distinct sound of a bottle of beer being opened with an opener. (That was back before twist tops were invented). Then the heels again down the stairs, and the jingle of the door.

When I heard you on a radio show last night on the way home from the drive-in it brought back some of these memories. I would love to hear your take on what I experienced – there is much more, but I know you are busy. I have only told a few people about any of this and I never really felt believed. However several friends who came to visit could feel the presence of the ghost and would not go through the house unaccompanied.

Would love to hear from you.

Alice

Dear Alice:

Ghosts are definitely creatures of habit. They are known for doing the same thing over and over. It always amazes me how stuck they can stay. In my book *Relax, It's Only a Ghost* I wrote about a ghost named Pearl who haunted a bar in Kentucky. I first met her in 1993 when I was shooting a segment for the TV show *Sightings*. She was sitting in a room in the basement, with her hands on her face, rocking back and forth. All she said over and over was "oh my head, oh my head." I tried talking to her but she just kept rocking and saying "oh, my head."

I discovered that two men had chopped her head off back in the 1890s and buried it somewhere in the vicinity of where the bar now stands. She and the two male spirits were totally stuck. They just hung out in the basement of this building, reliving events that had taken place over a hundred years ago.

So many ghosts I've met over the years have done the same thing, just repeating some scene from their life over and over again. When I stop and think about all the people I've met who live their lives in a similar fashion, it's easy to see how ghosts can become just as stuck as we can. Thanks for letter. Since you stated your experiences with your ghosts in the past tense, I trust all is calm on the ghost front. But if not, just remember, put your foot down and demand that they move on and they will.

Sincerely,

Echo

Hi Echo,

I just finished reading Relax, It's Only a Ghost *and I thoroughly enjoyed it. It's not very often that I feel comfortable sharing different spiritual encounters but reading the book brought back* memories of growing up on a dairy farm in northern Minnesota and the "weird" lifestyle I had. I say weird because not everyone's parents were hippies nor believed in the existence of spiritual beings. To this day my parents are still cultivating good spirits around the farm. My dad meditates and communes with the spirit guides on the farm to maintain the farm's health and well-being both on the physical plane and spiritual plane. My mom recalls stories of me going outside to play with the nature spirits. I have two stories for you:

1) When I was really young (maybe 5 at the most) I had a vivid dream with my guardian angel. I was frightened by the scary monsters in my dream and my mom told me to say the Lord's Prayer. I kept repeating it and my guardian angel showed up with a wonderful white light that kept the monsters away. I could see them but they couldn't get me! My guardian and I talked and walked around a very rocky landscape. We came to a ladder and I wanted to climb it, but he assured me it wasn't my time to go up yet. As a 5 year old, I was so curious to see what was up there but he wouldn't let me. He also has saved me from many potentially life-threatening accidents and still rescues me every now and then.

2) I have also had encounters with ghosts. When I was 7 my parents released a ghost who had been possessing a friend of theirs. I had my own encounter while in college when a ghost tried to enter my body while I was sleeping. I woke up in time to tell the being to leave me alone, that it wasn't welcome in my body. I could only think these thoughts, because, for some reason, I couldn't move my body or talk. As weird as it sounds, I was frozen in place in my bed until the being decided that it wasn't welcome. That has not happened again but if it does, I will be better prepared after reading your book.

I'm excited to pass this book around to some of my friends and my mom, who is very excited to read it.

Thanks again!

M

Dear M:

A thought came to me as I was reading your account of the ghost who tried to enter your body. The fact that you couldn't move your body or talk tells me that your soul was out of your body at the time this spirit paid you a visit. This is called astral projection or soul travel and since I've had quite a few letters regarding this, I'd like to address this next:

Astral Projection

When I was a little girl, I frequently had two kinds of dreams. One was that I was flying, and the other was that I was floating up by the ceiling in the corner of my room. I loved both of those dreams because they made me feel so free.

As I got into my teens, I started having a different kind of experience while my body was sleeping. I would stand at the end of my bed in the mornings and watch my mom trying to wake me up for school. It was such an odd experience because I couldn't figure out how I could be standing at the end of my bed and lying in it at the same time.

I could tell that my mom was having a heck of a time trying to wake me because my body appeared as still as a dead person. She eventually figured out that the only way to get me up was by throwing cold water in my face. I remember standing there, watching her come into my room with the glass full of water, but feeling powerless to do anything for my body. I was just frozen there.

There were other times when I was conscious of being my body and not being able to move. My mom would be yelling at me to wake up but I couldn't respond. I'd just lie there like an empty shell, wondering what was wrong with me.

Until I started taking psychic development classes I had no idea what was going on. But then my teacher told us about soul travel or astral projection. She explained that our souls leave our bodies at night and can travel anywhere they want to go. When our souls are out, our bodies are kind of shut down. They're still working, of course – but they usually lie very still. If we wake up while the soul is out, sometimes we can't open our mouths, speak or move our arms or legs.

Our soul is like a battery pack for our body. When it's out, the body will behave like a battery-operated toy whose batteries have been partially or completely removed. If all the batteries have been removed, the body won't move at all. If only a portion of the batteries have been removed, there will be some movement, but it's sluggish.

If you wake up in the middle of the night and you can't move parts of your body or can't speak, this simply means your soul has taken all of its energy to go out from the body. The best thing to remember is not to panic. Remind yourself that you read about soul travel in this book and that the experience is real, even if it's hard to understand. You aren't going crazy. You aren't having a stroke.

If your soul has left your body, it had someplace to go, so trust that there's a reason why your soul is gone, and tell yourself to be mellow. If you have to get out of bed, send a thought to your soul that you want it to come back in. When your soul is able to, it will come back into the body. It will either gently go back in or you will feel a jolt. You'll know you're back when you're able to open your eyes or move your body.

PLEASE UNDERSTAND THIS: Your soul has been coming and going from your body since the day you entered your body at birth. The fact that you're just now understanding it doesn't mean that your soul is now going to begin astral projecting. You don't have to do anything to prevent this from happening. It's a totally natural occurrence and your soul knows what it's doing. Some people are uncomfortable knowing about astral projection because they don't like knowing they can't control their souls, but it's important to remember that it's our soul that's actually in control.

Here is another letter from a young woman who experienced astral projection:

Dear Echo,

When I was around six and very sick, I was asleep in my bed when a friend of the family came to visit me. For some strange reason I was up in the air looking down at him talking to me and praying over me. I saw him lay a Snickers Bar on my bedside table, whisper a few things, and leave. When I woke up I thought I had just had a strange dream but then I looked on the table and there it was. He really had been there. I don't know why I have these experiences but it bothers me and I thought you might have a possible answer. Could you please help me?

Terri

Dear Terri:

Your soul was simply out of your body and that's how you were able to see your visitor, even though you were sleeping. I think children often have these kinds of experiences but don't talk about them because they don't know how to put them into words. It doesn't make logical sense to us that we are floating above our bodies, so we chalk it up to imagination. My hope is that as we open up to the idea of having a soul and looking at life from the soul's perspective, we'll open up to the idea of soul travel and eventually we'll be able to talk about these experiences. Just know that you're not crazy and you didn't make this up.

Sincerely,

Echo

Chapter Six

Getting Visited in Our Dreams

*W*henever I speak publicly, I end the lecture with questions from the audience. Invariably someone shares a dream about a loved one coming to them in a dream and they want to know if it's possible for our loved ones to communicate to us through dreams. The answer is a resounding yes. This is the most common way that our deceased loved ones communicate with us.

As I mentioned earlier, people who pass to the other side are usually free to travel to this side to check on us and see how we're doing. Often when they have a message for us, they'll come at night to communicate to our souls. The experience comes through to our conscious mind as a dream but we can tell if it's really a visitation by how "real" the dream felt. Regular dreams feel like a regular dream, but a visitation feels like a real experience.

Often only bits and pieces of the real experience come through to our conscious mind, though, so don't be surprised if a dream/visitation seems choppy. That's common.

Here's a letter from a reader who had a visitation with an old friend in her dreams:

Dear Echo,

Thank you for letting me share my ghost experience. It is a rare opportunity.

When I was in 6th grade I met a rebel hellion girl named Betty. Sparked similar rebel tendencies in me. My grandparents were raising me in a very disciplined, Christian environment. Betty's rebel acts were tastes of freedom to me. Favorite ritual, the cigarette. Our social link. Stolen cigarettes at that! We'd skip class and smoke at the baseball dugouts.

As time passed I found Betty lying to boys about her age. Like saying she was 15 when she was only 12. She'd sneak out at night and ride in older guys' cars. One night she rode up to my house with some boys and wanted me to sneak out, too. Something told me to stop there. I refused to go. I feared facing her at school the next day. Turns out my fears were unfounded. She wasn't at school. The car they were in was stolen and she got busted.

After reading about the incident in the paper my grandparents refused to let me see her again. The following year Betty became pregnant and moved to Florida. As years passed she became a faded, forgotten memory.

Then one night recently I was attending a party a good friend was giving for her sister's stepdaughter from Florida. The girl needed to be surrounded by loving friends. Her mother had been deeply entrenched with drugs, dealing and had committed suicide one day before her kids came home from school. They were numbed with shock.

I was shocked to find out that the girl's mother was my childhood friend Betty! Her daughter mirrored her beauty. I tried to console her daughter with childhood memories of her mom, but they were clouded with troubled times. Her daughter was bright and a good student. She was the same age as when I knew Betty. Eerie.

Then I had a dream. I was in Betty's childhood home, sitting in the living room. Betty appeared to me, asking how her daughter was. I told her she was fine, in good care, getting good grades. Betty was relieved. She walked down the hall out the back door and disappeared in a tree in the back yard.

I shared this vision with her daughter. Her daughter froze. Her grandmother had just planted a tree in the backyard as a family memorial to Betty. I was a bit shaken. Her daughter found some comfort in the idea that her mother could have peace in knowing she was okay. I realized that Betty and I still had a bond.

Echo, the dead have come to me in dreams since I was young (I'm 44). My ghost dreams never frighten me because they always happen as conversations in unique settings. But it isn't exactly something I can discuss freely with people.

I admire how you developed your skills. Do you think I could learn more on my own development? My experience with Betty and her daughter taught me to trust it. Thanks for letting me share.

Love,

D

Dear D:

Thanks for sharing your stories with me. What a great story about Betty's soul coming to you in your dream. I would imagine it gave her daughter a great deal of peace knowing that her mom was checking in on her. It gave me goose bumps as I read it.

Regarding your psychic development, yes, of course you can develop your psychic abilities. The key ingredients are time, patience and a group of people that you can practice with. There are some excellent books that can help you develop your gift. Check out the Recommended Book List at the end of the book.

Thanks so much for sharing your story about Betty.

Sincerely,

Echo

Here is another example of a loved one communicating through a dream:

Dear Echo,

My father passed away November, 2001 and I've been wondering how he's doing. One night I had a dream that there was a knock on my front door. It was so vivid, I actually felt like I got out of bed and answered the door. There was every one of my deceased relatives smiling at me. They said they wanted to reassure me that my dad was in heaven and doing great. At that point, I woke up because the dream was so "real." My question is that I want to know if this kind of thing really could have happened? Could that have really been my relatives? I felt so happy when I woke up, so I hope this was real. Thank you for your time.

Sincerely,

Connie

Dear Connie:

There's no doubt in my mind that this wasn't a real visitation from your relatives. That was pretty cool that they all came to reassure you. Thanks for sharing your dream Connie.

Sincerely, Echo

Dear Echo,

I was wondering if you feel very strongly about dreams foretelling the future or conveying information to the dreamer? I have many dreams that are very detailed, very vivid. But some of the information I have deciphered from my dreams has been different from what my aunt has learned, and I'm wondering if my dreams really aren't as informative or prophetic as I had thought. The main discrepancy I'm focusing on is the "afterlife." Both you and my aunt say that once you die, the life you go to is similar to the life you had here on Earth. That there are good spirits and bad spirits and your personality or characteristics in this life are pretty much the same on the other side. And that this is true no matter if you've died from old age or been murdered or if you've committed suicide. A dream I had, that seemed informative, started off with a cousin I'm very close with, shooting himself while he was talking to me on the phone. Then he reappeared to me as a ghost and showed me how wonderful the other side is and encouraged me to kill myself also so that I could join him. Then my deceased grandmother appeared to me, with two elderly women and told me not to kill myself, that my cousin had been lying to me.

Then they took me to the other side and showed me what it was really like if you kill yourself. It wasn't at all pleasant and it wasn't at all like my cousin had originally shown me. After I awoke, I thought I had had a real zinger of a dream but the information is in conflict with the information you and my aunt give about the other side and suicide. I was wondering if you could explain the difference to me, or if you could see where I was in error?

JB

Dear JB:

It's unclear to me as to whether or not your cousin is already deceased and that could have a bearing on the meaning of the dream but I don't want to get stuck here.

Your question about perception brings up a very good point, so I'll focus on that.

Several years ago I was talking to my therapist about an issue that took place in our family and I told her that my brothers and sister had a different perspective on it.

She told me that if all six members of my family went to the movies, we'd all be sitting in our own seat, watching the movie from the perspective of our own life experiences and that we could all walk away with a different meaning to the story. That was very helpful for me in understanding how people can have different perspectives on the same experience.

The same goes with different accounts that you'll hear or read about regarding the other side. We all see it from our own perception. Your grandma's perception of suicide is obviously different than your aunt's or my perspective. I've heard some psychics say that the place suicide victims go to is not pleasant as your grandmother says, but my perspective of what I've seen is quite different and varied. There are suicide victims hanging around in the astral plane because they don't feel worthy of going on to heaven and there are many suicide victims in a hospital on the other side getting the help they need. Your grandmother, aunt and myself could all be looking at the same place but each seeing it through our own perception, so everyone's definition of it may be different, but no one is in error.

Since your question is actually about dreams, and you say you have a lot of detailed, vivid dreams, I would suggest getting a good book on dream interpretation. There are many dream analysis books on the market, so ask your intuition to guide you to the right book. After awhile, you'll intuitively know which dreams are prophetic and which are messages for you. Our dreams can be wonderful messengers if we learn how to read them properly. Thanks for your letter.

Sincerely,

Echo

Chapter Seven

Ghostly Sounds Signal Death?

A few years ago, I was a guest on a morning talk show in Los Angeles called *The Mike and Maty Show* and they sent me to a haunted house in a small town outside of L.A.

The owners of the haunted house told the producer of the show that their ghosts make a lot of banging noise and they had recorded the sounds on audio tape.

When I walked through the house, I could feel strong male energy and could hear men laughing. Slowly, one by one, five male ghosts appeared to me. They told me they had all been construction workers when they were living and each had died in a work-related accident. They didn't know each other when they were living but found each other on the Astral Plane. Now they were spending their time going to different houses in this community, banging on people's walls. The homeowners played the tape recording of the banging noise and it had a distant, hollow pounding sound to it as if these ghosts were all still working at their construction job. I mention this experience because of these next two letters I received regarding a distant, hollow pounding sound. Because they both experienced the same sound, I'll answer their letters together.

Dear Echo,

I am wondering what you can tell me about an experience I had about eight years ago. It was a beautiful afternoon and I was cutting out some fabric on my living room floor. I was contentedly working away, when I heard a pounding noise that had a quality that made me freeze. It was a very hollow, distant sound that I knew was not normal.

My dog took no notice, which is definitely not normal! I was too afraid to look for a possible source, and put it out of my mind. No other frightening things happened that day. Approximately two weeks later, I was lying on the sofa one evening, watching TV, when I heard the same noise – five rapid raps. This time I made myself get up to explore, but could find no explanation. I kept it to myself, and thought no more about it until a few days after my father called with the news that my youngest cousin and her husband had been murdered. I guess I was too stunned to make a connection right away. I also felt some guilt, because I wondered if I was being called upon to prevent this from happening

What should I make of this?

Sincerely,

PJ

Dear Echo,

I caught you on WCCO AM Radio (Dark Star's program) a month or so ago and have been meaning to write you ever since.

I do have an unexplainable "experience" to share with you. It happened 32 years ago but I remember it clearly. A VERY LOUD knocking on the wall – starting from the top corner of the bedroom, sort of sideways from top to bottom, very loud at first then fainter as it ended. I'm not sure how many knocks – perhaps 10.

It happened twice. The first time I was asleep, alone – in the wee hours of the morning – and it literally knocked me out of my bed. (By "knocked" I mean I flew up and out.) It happened again – perhaps a couple of weeks or months later – when my husband was home. That time it knocked us both out of bed. We tried to find a logical explanation for it – but there was none. A few months later my husband was tragically killed.

I don't recall exactly how long it took me to realize it, but the knocking (so loud no one would ever forget it) must have been a warning about his impending death. It never happened again though I lived in that house and slept in that bedroom for another 4 or 5 years. I think it was his mother who had tried to warn him – she had died about 10 years earlier. They had been close.

Sincerely,

ML

Dear PJ and ML, and all of you out there who might be hearing this distant, hollow, pounding sound:

I want to reassure you that I've never known these sounds to be a precursor to someone's death. I'm not at all convinced that either of you were receiving a warning that your loved one was about to die. If they were warnings, I'd have to say they weren't very effective because neither of you knew what the knocking meant. It is curious that you both had this experience prior to someone's death, but more than likely, it was simply the shenanigans of a noisy ghost.

Sincerely,

Echo

Chapter Eight

Sex with Ghosts?

A few years ago I was a guest on Minnesota's top rated morning radio show, KQ92, with Tom Barnard and the Gang. Not being a morning person, I wasn't familiar with the show and had no idea what to expect when I showed up at the studio on Halloween morning. Over the years I had done lots of interviews about ghosts and thought I had heard every question imaginable until Tom Barnard began the interview by asking me if ghosts have sex. All I could think of was how was I going to explain all of this in ten seconds or less (they always tell us to keep the answers brief) so I looked him straight in the eye and said "yes, Tom, they do." By the end of that day, book sales of *Relax, It's Only a Ghost* had sky rocketed at Amazon.com for the state of Minnesota. People are fascinated with hearing about sexual encounters with ghosts!

As bizarre as this might sound to some of you, this kind of phenomenon really does happen. Over the last twenty-five years, I've had at least two dozen people tell me they've had some kind of sexual relationship with a ghost or in some cases, with the soul of someone (living) that they know. They're usually embarrassed to talk about it and many of them feel guilty because they enjoyed it. Several were married women who reported having sex with the soul of someone other than their husband.

One was a woman who called several times regarding a ghost problem she was having. I always got the strangest feeling about her and her ghost, but could never put my finger on what it was. My intuition told me not to waste my time going out to her house because it wouldn't solve the problem.

My secretary at the time was good at getting ghosts to move on, so she went to this woman's house and did a ghostbusting. When she returned she told me she had gotten rid of a male ghost but that she had a feeling he'd probably be back. She said she could sense a strong connection between the woman and her ghost but didn't know what it was. About two weeks later, the woman called to say her ghost was back. She wanted my secretary to come back and fix the problem, which she did – two more times.

But it didn't end there. My brother Michael, who is a very experienced ghostbuster, went to her house on another occasion, as did one of my advanced students who had taken over the ghostbusting part of my business. In every case, they thought they had gotten the ghost to move on but he would always come back.

Several years after all this started, the woman called me for a psychic reading. She told me that her ghost was still there and was now doing terrible, nasty things to her. She said she had spent all kinds of money trying to get rid of him but to no avail. I had a strong intuitive feeling that the timing was right this time and that I would finally be able to figure out what this was all about. So I agreed to do the reading.

The first image that came to me was of this woman's most recent past life. I could see that she'd been married to the man who was now haunting her home. My guides said this male spirit was very possessive of her and that her soul was also possessive of him. They said that this couple had been – and obviously continued to be – literally addicted to each other and that their souls had hoped that by coming back to Earth at different times they would break their addiction. But that's not how it was turning out. He found her and they are continuing their addictive relationship.

The guides said the only way she could get rid of this ghost was by standing up to him and telling him to leave her alone. They also said they seriously doubted she would do this because she obviously liked having him there. As far as the "nasty things" went, my guides said that the ghost was being sexual with her but that she was consenting to it. As you can tell, my guides weren't particularly sympathetic. They could see that she was choosing to be "victimized" by this male spirit and that nothing would work until she was really ready to give him up.

Something that I've learned over the years about this whole business of sex on the astral plane, is that a lot of times when people think they're having sex with a ghost, it turns out that they're actually having sex with the soul of someone living, but through astral projection. Here are two letters I received from women who were having this kind of soul-level sex:

Dear Echo,

I'm hoping you can help me with a problem I can't tell anyone else about. I feel kind of stupid writing to you because this does not involve a ghost. I think it's someone's soul.

The first time it happened was two weeks ago. I was sitting at my desk and I felt someone watching me. Then I saw the face and body of my girlfriend's husband, but it was see-through. He was transparent! I saw him float into my body and then I felt as if I was being made love to. I actually had an orgasm! Then he came out of my body and left. I sat there stunned. I couldn't even imagine making something like this up.

About four days later I was at home watching TV and it happened again, and again this morning it happened. Echo, what is happening to me? Am I hallucinating? Should I ask him if he realized what's happening? He and I have always flirted with each other, but because of my friendship with his wife, I'd never take it any further. I know I should be asking you how to stop this, but I like it. What should I do?

I can hardly look my friend in the eye for fear she'll know I'm having sex with her husband. Is this kind of thing even possible or am I losing my mind?

Smiling in Georgia

Dear Echo

I am a married woman with an unusual problem and I need some help. My neighbor and I have been attracted to each other for years and have even talked about having an affair but we don't want to do anything to hurt our spouses.

About three months ago, I started having these dreams where my neighbor and I are making love and I actually have a physical orgasm. The thing is, they don't seem like a dream. They seem like a real experience.

I haven't said anything to anyone about, this including my neighbor, but last night, at the end of a casual conversation about our day, his parting words were, "see you in your dreams." Echo, what did he mean? Does he have these dreams also? Is this real? What should I do? Am I cheating on my husband? Should I talk to my neighbor about this? What if I bring it up and he doesn't know what I'm talking about? Is there a way I can stop this from happening? I need help understanding all of this. Please write to me as soon as possible.

Sincerely,

Anne

Dear Smiling and Anne:

Both of you are not having "sex" with an earthbound spirit. These are examples of having "sex" with the soul of someone that you know. If this sexual experience is something you're enjoying, there is an agreement between your soul and the soul you're having "sex" with. I put sex in quotation marks because it's somewhat misleading. Since these are souls we're talking about, they obviously don't have physical body parts, but when souls "make love" it's more a coming together as one with a sexual intention and that's what creates the "orgasm."

If you are feeling guilty about having this kind of relationship with someone, and you want to stop it, you can, but you have to want it to stop. You can't act like a victim. You have to put your foot down (I sound like a broken record don't I?) and the next time you feel it starting to happen, firmly tell the soul coming into you to stop it right now and get out of your body. Then cross something on your body, like your arms or legs. Then do the Clearing Exercise in the Solutions Chapter. I also suggest having an out loud conversation with their soul and tell them you want these encounters to stop. Their soul will hear you.

As far as your question about cheating on your husband, only you can answer that one. Some clients I've talked to feel no guilt at all and others do. Maybe applying the Golden Rule will help you determine what's right or wrong for you. Ask yourself if you'd mind if your spouse was doing the same thing and see where that leads you.

Thanks to both of you for your letters.

Sincerely,

Echo

A word of caution: If this kind of thing is happening to you, don't *assume* you know who the person is and by all means don't confront them unless you're absolutely sure. I've learned that women are more consciously aware of these kinds of sexual encounters versus men, who tend to think they're just dreaming. I've had a few clients actually confront the man who they felt they were being sexual with, and the man had no idea what they were talking about.

If you feel violated like this next writer did, then you absolutely need to put your foot down and demand that it stop. Never allow a soul to victimize you.

Dear Echo,

I'm 21. I've experienced visits from family members who have passed on, but what I experience in my room at night is much different. I can hardly put it into words. My boyfriend thinks I'm crazy. Anyway, I have encountered a negative entity in my room almost every night. Now I can't even sleep there anymore. I'm too scared.

My parents are upset that I'm never home at night, but I just can't sleep in my own bed. Before, when I didn't have any other *place to sleep, I would either run to my parents' bed and sleep between them or make my mother lie with me in my bed until I fell asleep. I used to think I was experiencing sleep paralysis and I thought I could dismiss it as that. It had been a few years since I'd experienced this ghost, but recently it's back.*

There was one night in particular when the entity seemed the most aggressive with me. At the time I had a lover/friend who I was very passionate with. One night while I was sleeping in my bed I was awakened by what felt like immense pressure on my body. This had happened many times before, but this time the ghost seemed to be smarter than before. Everything was dark, but I could feel something powerful all around me and in front of me I saw the face of my lover/friend. Its shadow was dark but I could see that it was him. He started kissing me. I allowed him to, I relaxed a bit and then this thing that was kissing me deeply and that I believed to be my boyfriend began sucking the breath out of me, strongly. I was very scared.

Usually at this point I would start praying and that would allow me to be set free and allow me to run. Every other time I felt the presence holding me down, I would pray and be released in a cold sweat and able to speak and move. This time my prayers began in my own voice but after a few words I suddenly had this very deep-sounding male voice and couldn't move at all. I was more frightened than ever.

Ever since that night I have felt my breath taken again and again. The paralysis used to happen to me when I first woke up, but now my encounters begin as I turn off the lights and close my eyes.

I feel it through my entire body. Its engulfs me, pulling me down into the bed and I hear deep words that I cannot remember. I fight it, but I am so frightened.

These days if I have no choice but to sleep in my bed, I pray before the lights go out or I make the sign of the cross. The nights I do that, I sleep through the night.

I try to sleep with good thoughts. But whenever I am thinking of anything sexual my body is taken over. I know this has nothing to do with sleep, because one time I was thinking about someone sexually, not even with the intention to sleep, but I was in my bed in the dark and I felt the ghost on me again.

You say not to be frightened, that the spirits feed and grow from our Fear. If that's so, the ghost in my room must be huge by now because I am more frightened by it than anything, and I do not want to accept it. I DO NOT want to face it.

Can you tell me if my experiences are real, or if I'm just experiencing a trick of the mind?

There are some things I am leaving out of this story. My other grandmother, my father's mother, also used to live with us until she passed on. For twenty years the bedroom I'm now in was hers. My father once told me that she used to scream in the middle of the night. She would yell out in her native tongue, Spanish. I actually vaguely remember this. She would scream for someone to leave her alone and to get out. She would have dreams, or what she thought were dreams, that her bed was being levitated. This didn't happen all the time, but many times. As it is with me.

I have thought of blessing an item with my church and hanging it in my room. I have even thought of trying to get a priest to come in and bless it in hopes that he can cast out this unfriendly ghost. I don't know what to do but stay away. Can you help in any way?

TJ

Dear TJ:

There's obviously some very creepy spirit connected to that room and it has to be stopped. If you know a clergy person or a reputable ghostbuster in your area, I would definitely call them and ask them to come and clear out your bedroom. If neither of these are available, take an aggressive stand with the spirit. I want you to demand that it leave you alone. Burn a white candle in the room. Ask God to send in some healing angels to bless and clear the room and ask that they take the spirit home to the other side. Then ask them to fill up the room with the white light of protection so no one in your family is ever bothered again. Check back with me and let me know how this all works out, okay?

Thanks for your letter and don't be discouraged. This can and will stop. You just need to be very firm.

Sincerely,

Echo

Dear Ms. Bodine,

I am 23 and for the last 10 years, usually once a week during the time just before I fall asleep or take a nap, something very strange happens to me. I feel as though someone or something is sitting/lying on me. During the uncomfortable moments I am almost paralyzed and literally have to fight to sit up or even try to yell out. When this happens I can feel the bed indent due to pressure and my body being bent in strange ways. I also have felt as if I'm being pulled down the bed, hearing the sound of the rustling sheets pass my ears. Feelings of floating or being lifted or moved around. Also, embarrassing feelings of sexual arousal.

Ms. Bodine, I am no pervert, just a 23-year-old girl who sometimes is even afraid to nap during the day. This doesn't just happen at home. It happened when I was in Europe, too, and when I try to sleep on someone else's couch or something. Could there be a ghost following me? Or can you think of other explanations?

I know that when you fall asleep at night your nervous system shuts down, an explanation for the feeling of paralysis, but it happens within a minute. It used to frighten me, but now I let it do whatever to see what happens. After reading your book, Relax, It's Only a Ghost, I thought maybe something was entering me or playing around with me. Can you help me figure this out?

Sincerely,

Amanda

Dear Amanda:

It sounds like you're having out-of-body experiences, but I'm not sure what the sexual feelings are about since you didn't mention seeing or sensing a spirit around you. There is a possibility that your soul is having sex with someone and you're feeling it on a physical level.

Since this seems to happen anywhere, I would suggest that before you lie down to go to sleep, ask your spirit guides to watch over your body and protect you from any kind of invasion whatsoever.

If you do wake up while your soul is out of your body, simply send a thought to your soul that you would really appreciate it if it would come back because you're feeling anxious about it being gone. Then just be patient. It will be back before you know it.

Sincerely,

Echo

You should know that these sexual encounters don't just happen with women. I did a ghostbusting job in South Minneapolis involving a man and a female ghost. The ghost was very jealous of this man's fiancée and would sometimes push her out of bed when she spent the night. The man hired me to get rid of his ghost because his girlfriend thought he was the one pushing her out of bed and it was causing a lot of fights. When his girlfriend finally refused to stay overnight until the problem was fixed, he called me out of desperation.

At first I couldn't figure out what could possibly be pushing this woman out of bed. Then I met Sherrie. She was quite the ghost. Very arrogant, she thought she was hot stuff. She explained to me that the man who lived here was *her* boyfriend and that she loved him and liked making love to him at night. I remember wondering how I was going to approach this subject with the guy and even thought about completely leaving it out of the conversation, but I knew I had to bring it up. Sherrie was so sure that the man was in love with her, too. She told me she had to get rid of the girlfriend so she could have him all to herself.

I told the man everything that Sherrie had shared with me. He didn't seem all that surprised but he insisted that he didn't know her. He said that he had dreams of a female stranger making love to him at night. He used the words "it felt more real than just a dream" but couldn't imagine how it could be and just chalked it up to a vivid dream.

We finally got rid of Sherrie when he told her she wasn't welcome there anymore. He had to be very firm with her because she wasn't about to leave him on her own. I showed him where she was standing and told him to treat her like an intruder in his house. I instructed him to tell her that she had to leave and go to the other side. After he repeated this over and over, she finally did leave and never came back.

I talked to him about a month after the ghostbusting job and he assured me that everything was back to normal. He and his fiancée were doing very well and planning their upcoming wedding.

I wish I could explain to you all the comings and goings of ghosts, spirits and souls. I wish I could put it all in a neat little nutshell but there are just too many factors – too many different personalities, values, and perspectives from souls on many different levels. It's impossible to generalize why they do what they do.

The important thing is this: If you feel violated in any way by a ghost, you have to treat the ghost like an intruder and demand that it leave you alone. It must move on, and if it won't, ask God to send in an angel to take this ghost to the other side.

Chapter Nine

Visits from Animal Spirits

*I*n the summer of 2001, I was outside mowing the grass, deep in thought about a book I was working on, and wasn't paying much attention to what I was doing. Suddenly I heard a dog barking and it sounded really familiar. We don't have any dogs in our neighborhood that have that kind of bark, so I looked around to see where it was coming from.

Over to my right, about three feet away from me, was my dog Jessie, who had died in 1992. He was prancing around like he used to do and barking to get my attention. Without even thinking about it, I shouted out, "Hi Jess!" I was so happy to see him that for a quick second I thought about getting down on the ground and playing with him. He disappeared as quickly as he appeared but it sure left a big smile on my face.

Our deceased pets do have souls and do go on to the other side when they die. It's not uncommon for them to visit us just like our deceased relatives do. Just because they're out of sight, doesn't mean they're out of lives. The love we have for them continues on after death, just as their love for us continues on after death. Here are a couple of letters from people who have felt their deceased pets around them:

Dear Echo,

I saw a ghost when I was twelve. She was not in human form but came to me as a dog I had known. She looked like smoke but in such perfect form that I knew exactly who she was. She walked right in front of me, chased her tail looking for a place to sit, then sat herself down and disappeared. Poof! She was gone.

I have put myself on your mailing list and hope one day to attend one of your seminars. I enjoy your work. And I thank you for your time.

Sincerely,

TM

Dear Ms Bodine,

I want to share a story about our dear deceased Dharma Cat. It has been nearly three years since we lost Dharma Cat. When her kidneys shut down (in April of 1998) we euthanized her because she was in so much pain. When we returned home, our surviving cat, Lady Chelsea, would not go upstairs to the study where Miss Dharma had spent her last days.

At midnight, our closet door shook, just like she shook it when she was alive. Lady Chelsea Cat would not venture upstairs for nearly a week. Lady Chelsea took to hiding behind one of our large stereo speakers on the main floor. Over the next few days we both could hear Dharma Cat's collar tags tinkling. We "felt" her presence for nearly a week, then all was quiet until September of 1998.

I was saying goodbye to my husband at the top of the stairs, which lead to the garage. Out of the corner of my eye, I saw a grayish blur the same shape of Miss Dharma slinking along in the light. The shape I saw was just the very size of Dharma Cat! She was only there for a few moments. She had a stubby, short tail and slightly raised haunches as she had a little Manx in her. I noted that Lady Chelsea Cat was hiding in our bedroom closet, and would only venture out to eat or to use her litter box. She would only come to eat or use the box if one or both of us were with her. She actually relieved herself on our parrot Lady Jane's perch drop cloth, rather than go downstairs to the main floor. She acted terrified to be alone on the main floor of our townhouse.

All of a sudden Lady Jane Grey began calling out for Dharma. She had not called out to her since Dharma's passing. I asked Lady Jane if she could see Miss Dharma, and without hesitation, she said yes. (African Grey Parrots are some of the most intelligent parrots, and are known for their ability to understand and respond to questions.) I was at the dining table and I heard Dharma's collar tags tinkling. Lady Jane fluffed out all her feathers. I told my husband what had happened over lunch later that day. He seemed a little skeptical, but didn't disbelieve me. This happened on a Friday.

On the following Tuesday morning, my husband ran into the bedroom with great excitement. He woke me up saying "I just felt Dharma Cat brush against my leg as I was getting into the shower." Both of the bathroom doors were closed, and Lady Chelsea was asleep in my arms. We continued to "feel" Miss Dharma's presence for about ten days. Then, she seemed to fade. The next time she "came back" was in late November, when my husband became quite ill.

We seem to feel Miss Dharma's presence most clearly when George becomes ill, or is having a lot of turmoil in his life. I know that George loved Dharma very much. He still has a portrait of her on his desk, and a shrine dedicated to her on our main floor of the townhouse. I only hope that he isn't holding her here.

We are practicing Tibetan Buddhists, and believe in reincarnation. I hope that we aren't stopping the complete process of crossing on or over. I hope you enjoyed this story. I swear on my refuge vows as a Buddhist that every word of it is true. Thank you again for your book: "Relax, It's Only A Ghost." Good luck with all your future ghosting ventures. May you always be safe and free from harm.

Your friend,

PF

Echo,

In 1992 I decided to get a cat. My daughter named her Willie – only she could say why because Willie is a male name.

She was not a nice cat at all. The only time she would jump on your lap was in the winter time and only if you had an afghan over your legs. If you tried to pet her, she would jump down. She would never let anyone hold her and she never purred. I often accused her of being my mother, reincarnated, as my mother was not a nice person either. We had her about five years. But it came to a point that we had to call the humane shelter to come get her. She did not go peacefully. She put up a fight all the way to the van. She just got too mean and since she was that way she had to be put to sleep. So I believe she got stuck here. Too mean to leave.

I can't really say what the exact time frame was, but a few months after her death she came back. When she was alive she always slept on my bed at the foot, on the left corner. That's the only time she'd get near anyone. One night just after I went to bed I felt something jump up on the bed at that left corner. I lifted my head to see what it was but didn't see anything. I thought I just must have imagined it. A few nights later I was awakened when something jumped on that corner again and began kneading the bed. I pushed with my left foot at the covers and it stopped. I then realized it was Willie. She was back with us in spirit. This went on for maybe 2 years.

Then one morning as I was coming out of sleep I felt her jump on the corner, walk across my legs to the back of me and knead the covers next to my back. I said "Hello, Willie." The kneading stopped and she never came back to visit again. I think she just wanted me to acknowledge she was there.

The story is not over. In April 1999 I moved into an apartment. I brought that bed with me but found out that it was too big (queen size) for the new bedroom. I had not much room for anything else but it. So I decided to buy a day bed for myself and give my sister the queen size bed. She ended up only taking the headboard and the frame. About a month after I gave it to her, her son got shot during a robbery and needed to recuperate from surgery at her house, so they got him a hospital bed and set it up in the living room. I should say at this point that my sister has a cat of her own.

After his second night there, my nephew got up in the morning and said to his mother, "Did you know you have a ghost cat in the house?" She asked him to explain. He said he was in bed trying to go to sleep when he felt a cat jump on his bed. He lifted his head to look but nothing was there, so he thought it must have been their cat, but when he got up to go to the bathroom he saw that it couldn't have been her. She was sound asleep on her rug in the bathroom corner.

After that night, several times my sister has felt a cat jump on her bed at the left corner at the foot of the bed. When she looks, no one is there and her cat is either sleeping on the floor beside her or in the bathroom. She has come to the conclusion that Willie followed the bed, partly because her cat has started to act really strange. The cat will be sleeping in the middle of the living room floor and wake up startled, then start hissing and running like mad all around the house, like she's chasing something or something is chasing her. Once my sister said aloud "Willie, you're welcome to stay here but you have to leave my cat alone or leave." Her cat settled down right away. But it's still happening to her cat, and as of two nights ago, something is still jumping on the bed. There's my story. I hope you enjoyed it.

Ms. L

Dear Ms. L:

Thanks so much for your letter. I certainly did enjoy it and can relate to it as well.

Shortly after we adopted a five year old gray and white Persian cat named Susie, I started experiencing the same things you talk about in your letter. Two or three nights a week, I feel a cat jump up on my bed. Then it walks around my body and does the kneading thing. When I open my eyes to pet Susie, she's nowhere in site. At first I wondered if it was Susie's soul just playing around while her body slept but last week I saw the spirit of an orange Tabby run out of my room. It scared the heck out of me! I have no idea who this cat is, but it's interesting that she showed up shortly after my boyfriend and I started discussing the idea of getting another cat for Susie to play with!

I have heard from several cat owners that report similar kinds of cat spirit activity after their beloved pet dies. I really believe their cats are simply letting them know they're still there. It's so comforting to know our pets live on, isn't it?

Sincerely,

Echo

This next letter is a little different in that it's a question about whether or not our deceased loved ones might choose to communicate through an animal:

Dear Echo,

My mother-in- law died three years ago. She was a painter and often painted Great Blue Herons. After she passed away my father-in-law saw a Blue Heron at the cemetery just looking at him. It stood there for a while and then flew away. Two weeks later, my father-in-law was looking out his window and saw the Blue Heron again. Then my husband was coming home one night and the Blue Heron was standing off to the side of the road, about ten miles from the cemetery. We live in a part of the country that doesn't have Blue Herons. Do you think this could have been the spirit of my mother-in-law in the form of the Blue Heron?

I just heard you on the radio tonight. I have wondered about this for a long time.

Thank-You,

E.G.

Dear E.G:

I've heard so many great stories from people over the years who have wondered if a deceased loved one might be trying to reach out to them through an animal.

I have no doubt that your mother-in-law is trying to connect with you to let you know she's around. And what a clever idea – and one that would definitely get your attention – to choose her favorite bird. Thanks so much for sharing your story with me.

Yours,

Echo

Our deceased loved ones, our spirit guides, and our guardian angels do all kinds of creative things to get our attention and let us know that we're not forgotten, we're not alone, and that we're being watched over.

If one of your deceased loved ones had an animal or symbol that was special to them and they're trying to communicate to you, it would be very likely that they would choose some kind of replica of that animal or symbol to get your attention. Many people chalk these experiences up to coincidence, but believe me, these aren't just chance happenings. Our deceased loved ones delight in knowing that we know they're nearby. We just have to pay attention and keep an open mind. A good example is the psychic medium John Edward on his television show *Crossing Over.* Many times when John is giving information to an audience member from a deceased loved one, the information doesn't click right away. John tells the audience to set aside their preconceived idea's of how their loved one *should* be communicating and be open to whatever information they're able to bring through. This is what I mean when I say we have to pay attention.

Chapter Ten

www.ghoststudy.com

*I*n October, 2000, I was contacted by a man named Jim (real name) about his website, www.ghoststudy.com. He said he wanted to do something fun on the website for Halloween and asked if I'd be open to answering questions that people sent in regarding ghosts and things. It sounded like fun so we decided to do it.

He sent out a message and invited people to send in their questions. We received lots of good questions and I thank Jim for giving me permission to share those questions and answers with you here. Check out his website. He's got all kinds of information about ghosts and some great pictures as well. Here are a few of the questions and answers:

Q: What is your stance on exorcism?

A: I believe negative souls can possess us and I also believe they can be exorcised by a competent shaman or healer of some type (including clergy). I have only done about four de-possessions myself. It's interesting work!

Q: There are specific meters that are used for detecting ghosts, are these really useful on a ghost hunt?

A: If a ghost hunter can't see the ghosts, these meters can be helpful.

Q: Why are ghosts selective about who they interact with or reveal themselves to?

A: Ghosts are actually not selective about who sees them or who they interact with. They'll interact with or appear to anyone that can see or hear them and they can tell by the color of our aura's who's psychically open.

Q: Just how do ghosts communicate with us? Please tell the details of how to do it! Why do they do it so infrequently? Why don't they clarify their partial messages to us?

A: Ghosts are made up of energy that is not easily seen by the human eye. Once they leave the body, their energy is of a different vibration or frequency, which is very light. We're used to the heavier energy here on Earth and used to hearing the clear, audible communication we humans use when we speak to each other. Spirits/souls/ghosts communicate by thinking. They send thoughts. It's such a light vibration that even when they are communicating, most of us are not aware of it.

Souls are always trying to communicate to us. Receiving those messages has a lot to do with our state of mind at the time, our ability to hear clairaudiently, our beliefs, how relaxed we are, etc.

They think in full messages. We're the ones who receive them partially, depending upon our ability to hear.

Q: When dealing with a spirit you often advise that people protect themselves with a prayer (white light, sage, candles, etc) from whatever religion they follow. Why do we never consider the religion of the spirit? If it is a spirit of a person that was Jewish in life, why would a Catholic blessing work?

A: This is an important question and I'm glad you asked it because people assume ghosts react to crucifixes or other religious symbols and it's been my experience that they don't. Most ghosts could care less about these things. Lighting white candles, saying certain prayers or wearing a crucifix – these are things we do for *our* benefit to help us feel safe and protected. People also think that sage gets rid of ghosts, but it doesn't. It clears a place of negative thought forms or feelings but does not get rid of spirits. I've seen ghosts leave a room filled with sage smoke, only to return when the smoke has cleared out.

I think the reason ghosts aren't affected by crucifixes is that they don't see themselves as evil. It doesn't occur to them that the reason the homeowner is hanging them all over the house or wearing a cross and saying prayers is because of *THEM*. They think of themselves as regular people and might think the crucifixes are to protect the family from demons and something along that line but certainly not to protect the homeowner from *them*.

An interesting piece I've learned about ghosts is that the majority of them who do have religious beliefs believe that God is a punishing Deity who will send them to Hell once "he gets his hands on them" which is why they choose to remain earthbound.

Like I said, lighting candles, saying prayers and wearing

crucifixes or something religious is for our benefit and has little effect on the ghosts.

Q: I was wondering, when you "sense" the presence of a ghost, are they most likely in orb-form or are they already an apparition-form by this time?

A. I see them as a formed person, but in photographs they often appear as round balls of energy which is what an orb is.

Q: Do you have any opinions on whether spirits who were mentally ill when they were in human form carry mental illness into the spirit realm? If so, have you had any personal experience with such a spirit or ghost? Thank you!

A: Yes, I've met some ghosts who suffered from mental illness when they were living and yes, it can carry over into death.

Several years ago my brother and I went on a ghostbusting job where there were several spirits that had been mentally ill when they were alive. The homeowner called us because her 8-year-old daughter wouldn't sleep in her own room. The woman didn't tell us that her daughter said there were people in her bed because she wanted to see what we came up with first. We walked through the entire house and when we got to the little girl's room, we saw seven spirits all laying on the little girl's bed. They seemed totally out of touch with what was going on. We asked our guides what was going on and they said that these souls had lived and died in a mental hospital and remained earthbound because they wanted to stay in the area they were familiar with. They said the hospital had been located where these people's home now stood. We told the woman what the guides said and she confirmed that there had been an insane asylum on their property a long time ago. That's when she told us that her daughter refused to sleep in her own bed because of "all the people laying on it." It was pretty pathetic. These souls seemed so lost and that's why they clung to each other and stayed in the safety of this little girl's bedroom. We did get someone from the other side to take them home, and the mother later told us the daughter was sleeping sound in her own bed again.

If you sense you have such a ghost, or are worried about someone you know who has passed and suffered from mental illness, be sure to say their name out loud and tell them to look for the white light and go to the light. They will be taken care of when they go over the other side.

Q: Can you give a list of some signs that would help a person with no psychic abilities figure out if their house was haunted? Thank you.

A: Tapping or knocking on the walls

Doorbell rings and no one is there

Radio and or television goes on and off by itself

The sound of footsteps

Sounds of breathing

Water faucets being turned on by themselves.

Voices are heard and no one is there

Music is heard with no obvious source playing it.

Books or other material possessions being knocked off shelves

Clothes thrown out of closets

Waste paper baskets turned upside down

Burners turned on the stove

A definite cold spot in the room and no draft or window

Lights flickering on and off

Material possessions moved from room to room

A white or grayish hazey object floating through a room

Something touches you but no one is there

A feeling of someone sitting down on your couch or bed

Children claiming they can see someone and you can't

Something pulling your hair or tugging on your clothes

A feeling someone is watching you

Your house has been for sale for a long time and no one will buy it.

Q: Are ghosts capable of making people sick or able to cause their deaths on purpose?

A: After all that I've seen over the years, I wouldn't rule out anything anymore. I guess these things are possible. But let me say that in the 35 years I've been dealing with ghosts I've never known one to cause someone's death. I have met some that take energy from the people who live in the house they're haunting, which can run down their immune system, and *that* can cause sickness, but I've never known of a death by ghosting.

Q: I have always played with Ouija boards. Last June a friend of mine and I were talking on the Ouija board and had a very miraculous experience. It said it was an angel and was here to help me, which to this day I fully believe was the case. She said she was channeling through my friend. She ordered that we break the Ouija board and purchase an Angel board. At that time I did not even know what an Angel board was. I finally located one online, bought it, and continued talking to her. She helped my life a lot.

My friend has since moved so I have had no contact with her, but recently my 10-year-old son and I pulled out the angel board and away the planchette went! Stronger than ever!!!! Very scary. It claims

to be another angel but it is very very different from the one that my
friend and I would talk to. This one swears and says that it is chan-
neling through my son. It always says, "Alex isn't here." (Alex is my
son.)

To get on with the story, we were talking to it the other night. It
swore so I yelled at it. It said I was mean and it began to cry. It con-
tinually kept on spelling C-R-Y, C-R-Y, C-R-Y, C-R-Y, C-R-Y reallllly fast.
Next thing I know my son is crying hysterically. I asked him why and
he said "I don't know." Okay. Now there have been many things
going on in my house voices, noises, items disappearing and so forth.

I need some help here. I don't know if my son could possibly be
possessed or if the thing just decided to move in. But it is bad. I don't
know if you deal with things like this and it is a hard thing to tell friends
about. They think I am nuts! Please, if you can help me at all please
respond. Thank you.

A: Lisa, I'm glad you asked this question, because the whole
business of playing with the Ouija Board is very dangerous if people don't know what they're doing. Most people buy them to play
with and be entertained, but some of these earthbound spirits
love to freak people out and they usually will do so through the
Board. No matter if it's a Ouija or Angel Board, unless you can
hear and see spirit, you don't know who is coming through.

Perhaps you did have an angel during the first encounter which
is rather uncommon. I've never met an angel who works through
one of those boards, but that doesn't mean it doesn't happen.
My experience with the board is limited but it was frightening
enough that I quit using it.

I want you to throw away the Angel Board (preferably burn it).
Then I would strongly suggest you get a copy of my book *Relax,*
It's Only a Ghost and read and carry through on the step-by-step

instructions of how to get rid of a ghost. I want you to walk through your house and demand that all earthbound spirits get out of your house now. I want you to call in the Squadron, which is a group of former ghosts who will come and clear your house out of negative spirits. Then, do not talk about the spirits while in the house for at least three days. Let them be on the other side for a while.

Next, I want you to ask for a real angel to come to your home and surround it in white light, sealing up the borders of the house so that no more intruders will come in. Then I want you to get some sage and burn it. I want you to run the smoke up and down your son and ask that he be cleared of any negative energy NOW. Children are very vulnerable and shouldn't be playing with any of these kinds of boards. They don't need to be open to this kind of energy.

Remember, Lisa, not to act afraid. Put your foot down and demand that any unwelcomed earthbound spirits in your home leave NOW. That should do it!

Chapter Eleven

How to Communicate with Spirits

$\mathcal{I}$ would have to say the most common question I'm asked is how to communicate with spirit guides, guardian angels, deceased loved ones, and ghosts and the answer is very simple. Just talk to them. Out loud or silently, whichever you prefer. My personal preference is out loud, so that they're very clear that I'm talking to them. Hearing their answers is a whole other thing and that's the part that's tough for us because we're used to hearing audible voices when someone is talking to us. Spirits communicate to us through thought and that's why spirit communication can be difficult. There is a book called *How To Communicate with Spirits* by Elizabeth Owens that I highly recommend if this is something you're interested in.

Dear Ms. Bodine,

I think I have a ghost or spirit in my house. I see, feel, and hear things. I've seen a small light moving around, and also something I can't explain that was floating over my dog. Whatever it was,

my dog woke up and took off out of the room. The babies' toys go off for no reason, I hear the dogs' toys moving around even though the dogs are sleeping next to me, and when I go downstairs to investigate the toys will be in the middle of the room. Other things have happened. I was wondering if there is a way I could talk to the ghost to see if it's real or if I'm going crazy.
Thank You.
P.S. I enjoyed listening to you on Dreamland.

Dear Writer:

I want to reassure you that the symptoms you describe are characteristic of someone trying to communicate with you and that you're not going crazy or making it up. I don't want to jump to conclusions that it's a ghost. It could be a Guardian Angel, a spirit guide, or a deceased loved one trying to get your attention. The light that you mention indicates that this is a positive spirit and not one that's earthbound.

As far as how to talk to it, you can talk out loud or silently. If you decide to think to them, start out with a really direct thought, like "to the spirit that is in our house." These spirits don't hang around listening to our thoughts all day, so you need to direct your thoughts so they'll know you're sending them their way. Remember, this is just like having a communication with anyone. Tell them that you would like to establish a more conscious contact with them and that you'll pay more attention to the things that go on around your house.

Several years ago when I was trying to develop a conscious relationship with my spirit guides, I did just what my teacher suggested. I told them I wanted to get to know them. Get to know when they were around. I wanted to know their names and be able to hear them if they had a message for me. I stayed with it. I didn't just say it once and leave the rest to them. I told them often that I wanted a good relationship with them, and as my fear went away, they were able to break through the veil that separates their world and ours, and I was able to hear them and see them.

Just remember to be patient. If it was easy for them to communicate with us (so that we were conscious that it was them), they'd be doing it all the time. Thanks for writing.

EB

Ms. Bodine,

I heard you on the radio Sunday night. I have always been interested in your area of expertise, but have also been very skeptical. To my knowledge I have not seen a ghost or had an experience like the ones discussed on the radio. Having said that, I also know that there are just as many nuts and con men out there looking to make a buck on anything.

My question to you is this, how would someone like me go about experiencing something like this? I am not really sure that I would not be frightened to death if it happened, but my curiosity would certainly like some answers. How do you separate the fact from the fiction, the real from the imagination?

Thank you in advance for your time and I enjoyed listening to you.

Dear Writer:

Great question. How do we separate fact from fiction when we're dealing with a realm of existence most people aren't aware of, and how do we distinguish between the quacks and the real deal?

I always rely on my inner voice to help me know who and

what I can trust. It's always steered me in the right direction regarding authors, speakers, seminars, books and anything else for that matter.

Several years ago a well-known speaker was coming to Minneapolis. Everyone I knew was going to go see him, as he had become quite popular in the alternative community. My intuition loudly told me to stay away and not waste my money or my time on his teachings or predictions because he was not what he was claiming to be. My head argued back, saying that "everyone is going," but my inner voice stood firm, insisting that it would be a waste of time. In spite of everything my intellect and my friends were saying, I listened to my inner voice. As time passed it came out that this person was not as much on the up and up as everyone had thought.

I guarantee you if you listen to your inner voice, you'll never be steered wrong and it will always indicate what's fact and what's fiction, no matter what area you're dealing with.

Regarding your question about how someone like you would go about experiencing "something like this," I'm not sure what you mean by "like this."

I'm going to assume you mean seeing ghosts since that's what I talked about on Dreamland. You can check your local area and see if there are any known haunted buildings, tours to haunted places, or museums, or log onto www.ghoststudy.com, which lists haunted places by location. You can also check my website, www.echobodine.com, for other ghost links and see where they lead you.

Once you find some places to investigate, go in and sense if you can feel or see a presence. My guess is that your intellect is probably blocking any ghosts from actually being able to communicate with you, so you might have to go in search of them rather than wait for them to search you out, if this is something you really want to do. Because you're skeptical, the process might take a little longer, so you need to be patient. I would also read up on the paranormal (see Recommended Book List) so that you have as much information as possible. It will help you be aware of a lot of things that many brush off as coincidence.

Thanks for writing, and good luck in your pursuits of the paranormal.

Sincerely,

EB

Dear Echo,

I was hoping you could help me. For the last two weeks my daughter's T.V. has been coming on when no one is up in her room. It comes on every night at 8:48 p.m. When she shuts it off, it's always on a channel, but when it comes back on by itself it is no longer on any channel. There is also no sound. We have seen some images but nothing real clear. I believe it is my mom and grandma trying to tell me or my daughter something. We just can't figure out what it is.

If you could give me any suggestions or questions I can ask it would be greatly appreciated. Thank you for you time.

GS

Dear GS:

I would keep it very simple. Tell whoever it is, *out loud,* that you would appreciate them being very specific about what they want. Tel them if they can't do that, then you want them to leave your daughter's TV set alone. Be firm and clear with them about what you want and if, after a couple of days, nothing becomes clear to you and the TV set is still going on at 8:48, tell them they need to move on and stop bothering you. Then I would call in the Squadron and ask them to take the earthbound spirit out of there. (See the Solutions chapter for further information about the Squadron.)

Chapter Twelve

Spirit Pictures

Spirit photos are always fascinating to me. Whether they're orbs (energy balls), streaks of energy, hazes, semi-shaped forms or full-fledged pictures of a soul. Unfortunately, catching spirit energy on film is not easy. I'd be curious to know just how many rolls of film my brother and I have gone through to capture a ghost's picture.

I literally pleaded with my guides to make something show up on film so I could prove to the skeptics once and for all that ghosts were real, but my guides told me it wasn't up to them. It had to do with the amount of energy the ghosts have in order to make themselves visible. A story comes to mind of a ghostbusting job we went on several years ago. A local newspaper was doing a story on us for Halloween. In the afternoon of the gig, my spirit guide appeared to me and told me to be sure and take my camera because the ghost at this house was going to make a point of materializing for us! I called the newspaper and asked if they were bringing a photographer and they assured me they were. About an hour before I left for the job, my guide said that the photographer wasn't going to make it and to be sure to bring my camera. I called the reporter and asked if there was a problem with the photographer and she said that he was all set to meet us there. When I got off the phone, my guide said to bring my camera anyway! Well, I didn't have any film in it and didn't want to deal with getting some, so off to the job I went, without camera in hand.

The first thing the reporter said when she got out of the car was that the photographer was called away on an assignment and wasn't going to make it and did I feel like an idiot for not trusting my guide. We went into the house and began looking around. We heard a noise at the stairway and looked over to see what it was. There, fully materialized in a beautiful white light was the male ghost that haunted this house. He looked right at me and said "take my picture" and I told him that no one had a camera. His comment back to me was that he told "them" to tell me that he would be appearing for the camera. Oh, I was so mad at myself. Every one of us was in awe of this very clear and glowing spirit. He seemed to be a nice guy and wanted to do whatever he could to convince the skeptics he was for real. He also made it clear to me that he didn't want to move on. That he was "taking care of the house" for these people and certainly wouldn't let any harm come to it. After seeing him, the homeowner was glad he was there, so we left him be. He did say he would move on when he was ready, but that he wasn't ready to let go of the house yet.

(I didn't mean to get side tracked, but I figured you'd want to know about him. Back to spirit photos.)

Something interesting I've learned over the last couple of years about spirit photos is that even with amazing pictures that prove spirits exist, the skeptics still try to find reasons why they aren't real. They come up with excuses like "the shutter was left open" or "it was too cold outside and that's what created the energy in the picture."

A few years ago I was very privileged to be shown some amazing pictures taken by a policeman at the scene of a fatal car accident that killed a 16-year-old boy. It took me years to convince him to let me have a copy of them so that I could show people I had proof that souls really exist. I was so sure that all I needed was the pictures, but shortly after acquiring them, I discovered a lot of resistance in people about accepting them.

Even though I can't show you the pictures (my publisher said it would be too costly), I would like to describe them for you. First, here's a letter from another policeman about some pictures he took:

Dear Ms. Bodine,

I'm a cop. The other night I went to a homicide and the sergeant took a couple of Polaroid pictures of the victim. In one picture the victim is just lying on the ground. In the other photo you can see a solid tube of light coming out of the victim's mouth and going off the picture. There are no other light distortions and the picture was taken at the same time as the other photo, which had no distortions. I spoke with Bob, the cop who took those pictures you have of the soul above the car and the tube of light from the Polaroid looks similar to the light coming from the back of the face in his pictures.

I spoke with my Sergeant and gave him your e-mail address. Hopefully he will get in contact with you.

Dear Officer:

Thanks for your email. It's cool to know that the pictures your Sergeant took are similar to the pictures the other policeman took. I learned a lot from those pictures. As we continue to improve our technology, I would imagine we'll be able to get some amazing pictures in the future. I haven't heard from your Sergeant yet, but look forward to it.

Sincerely,

Echo

Police Photos

Several years ago a couple of women came to me and asked if I could interpret some energy that showed up in some routine pictures that a policeman had taken at a fatal car crash (when the officer was looking in the camera, he saw nothing unusual. It wasn't until they were developed that the energy showed up).

When I first looked at the pictures, I had no idea what I was looking at, but when I opened up psychically and asked my guides, they explained everything to me.

The first picture was of the young man who was killed in the accident. There was a picture of his body lying in the front seat and he looked as if he was sleeping. There was a stream of energy coming out of his mouth. It was white, yellow and red. It zigzagged around and appeared almost like what we think electricity looks like. In the next picture, the policeman took a picture of him from the back seat and there were streams of this energy coming out of his back. In the third picture, these streams of energy were all over the picture, so much so that the policeman couldn't remember what he had taken a picture of. The picture looked like that spray confetti the kids have at birthday parties. It was all over the picture in the colors white, yellow and red.

In the last picture the cop stood back and took an overview of the car and surrounding area and when the picture was developed, you could see the energy coming together above the car to form the boy's soul. It's an actual picture of his head above the car yelling NOOOOOOOOOO. He looks very angry and it stands to reason that he would be angry, because he was 16 years old, on his way to a rock concert with his friends.

When I first looked at the pictures, I had no idea what all this energy was, because up until that point, I was under the impression that when the soul came out of the body at death, it came out in one piece. I probably got this impression from seeing ghosts as whole people. But my guides told me that his soul was coming out of his body in fragmented pieces, which they explained is not uncommon. They said he didn't want to be dead, and it was taking time for him to adjust to what was going on, so his soul was coming out in strands of energy. These pictures, by the way, were being taken within twenty minutes of the accident.

The other amazing part of the picture was that there was a picture of a dog's soul sitting next to the car. One of the women told me that the dog in the picture had been this boy's dog and had died about a year before the accident. The dog was just sitting there, looking like he was watching the policeman take the picture. It was amazing.

There was also an image of two male spirits in the last couple of pictures, and my guides told me that they were this boy's spirit guides coming to take him on to the other side. So for those of you who might be wondering if he stayed earthbound as a ghost, he didn't!

Chapter Thirteen

Ghostbusters

To Ms. Echo Bodine,

I'm writing to you because, like you, I've seen ghosts all my life. When I first see them, they appear solid and living. In fact I'm never sure they're ghosts until they talk to me. Then when I respond people around me look at me funny because they think I'm talking to myself. That's when I know. These ghosts don't seem to realize that they're dead.

Once I even shook hands with one of the ghosts. His hand felt normal. Two men next to me thought I was hallucinating and made some jokes out loud about it. They asked me who I was talking to and I answered, thinking maybe they had a problem. The men went into the grocery store ahead of me and told the checkout women that I was talking to ghosts. They looked shocked when they asked me questions about what the ghost looked like and I described their store manager to a tee. The manager had been killed in a car wreck two weeks earlier. I'd seen him there before but I didn't know he'd died until they told me.

I don't always see ghosts. Sometimes I just sense them. There was this one time when I went into a music store and got this feeling that something didn't want me near the acoustic guitar section. I went over anyway and felt a large hand on my left shoulder. I turned around in a complete circle but there was nobody there, except a couple talking to a salesman. They all stopped talking and looked at me like there was something wrong with me. I didn't say anything and walked off.

Anyway, the main reason I wrote is to ask you, is it very unusual for someone to see ghosts as solid and physically alive looking? When I see psychics on shows like Sightings or Paranormal Borderline they usually just seem to get impressions about the ghosts, like they get a letter or the name Sam or something, but I can just see them and walk up to them and ask them questions and get answers, if they want to talk.

If you could give me any advice about all this, what to do with my talent, if it's very unusual or not, or anything else, I would really appreciate it. As you know, there aren't a whole lot of people I can talk to.

Thanks for your time!

JCR

Dear JCR:

I'm not quite sure if you're seeing these ghosts with your third eye (psychic eye) or your human eyes but the fact that no one else sees them but you tells me you're seeing them with your third eye, which means you have clairvoyance, or the gift of psychic sight.

You sound very level-headed and I believe you could be of great service to a lot of these stuck, earthbound spirits. If ghostbusting is work that you would like to get into, I would suggest reading *Relax, It's Only a Ghost* because I want you to have as much information as possible before getting into this whole business because it's best to be prepared for whatever might come up.

Once you feel confident in your ability to get the ghosts to move on, I would suggest going to your local new age bookstore and introducing yourself, in person, to the owners and managers. Tell them that you have the ability to see ghosts and if they need a ghostbuster, you are available.

I would like you to stay in touch with me and let me know how it's going. Time will tell if this is your calling, but it certainly sounds like you've got the gift of seeing ghosts and you don't have any fear about it, which is an important ingredient in being a ghostbuster. Let me know if you decide to do this work. Thanks for your letter John.

Dear Echo,

Hi. I'm a seventeen-year-old senior in High School. For the last five months I have been obsessed with learning and researching every little thing that I can to learn about ghosts. Everything from how to hunt for them, how to take pictures of them, the equipment to use. It's all so interesting to me.

My friends think that I'm crazy, but what do you expect? It is weird. It would absolutely be a dream come true if I could meet with you and you could tell me if I could ever help ghosts go to the other side or something. We're both in Minnesota so I thought it would be convenient.

First off the bat, I wanted to tell you that I am so fascinated with you and your abilities, not just your way with the ghosts, but the way you present yourself. You are so real and true and the way that you write is just brilliant. You are a true role model to me. I have researched your website from top to bottom, fascinated with everything. I want to become a ghostbuster and I don't really know what that takes, that's why I'm writing you. It just hit me one day that this is what I wanted to be. I know that ghostbusting doesn't pay much if anything at all, but for some reason that doesn't matter. I just feel like God one day decided he wanted me to help him out, but it would really help me if I knew just why I started obsessing over wanting to be a ghostbuster just one day out of the blue. It's just all so weird to me.

If my feelings were totally wrong about being a ghost buster and/or being spiritually blessed, I would like to become a photographer for ghosts, a camera woman, those people who use all the expensive equipment to detect ghosts.

I would like to know what classes I should take in college to help me accomplish my dream. Also, one thing in Relax, It's Only a Ghost *that caught my eye is that you mention students a couple of times. What exactly do I have to do to become a student of yours?*

Thanks for your time.

To my Minnesota neighbor and all you people out there who would like to become ghostbusters:

I receive so many letters from people who want to know how to become a ghostbuster. I remember how excited I felt at being able to help ghosts go to the other side, so it's always fun to read these letters and be reminded of that enthusiasm.

First, there are two kinds of ghostbusters – the kind who, like me, can see and hear them and know they are souls who need help moving on and the kind we see on TV with their scientific equipment that registers ghosts as energy. I know this equipment really does register their energy because I've seen it with my own eyes, but I'm not sure what these people do to get ghosts to move on.

So you have a couple of choices here. You can take psychic development classes and develop your psychic sight (clairvoyance) and hearing (clairaudience) and/or you can pursue the more scientific approach. You can call your local colleges or check them out via the Internet and see if they have a parapsychology department and if they do, what they offer in the way of classes.

You could also surf the Internet about ghosts and ghostbusters and see what's available out there. You could study ghost pictures to find out what kinds of photography was used. A lot of the ghost pictures I've seen were taken with a 35 mm camera and regular film.

My advice is to read as much as you can about ghosts so that you have as much knowledge as possible. Ask your intuition to guide you to the right books because some of them are kind of goofy. Some people write about ghosts as if they are all demons, and that's not what my experience has been at all.

Check with ghostbusters in your area to find out if you can apprentice with them. Three of my former students who are now doing my ghostbusting jobs all went with me on several ghost jobs to learn from me first hand how to do this work. Once I felt confident in their abilities, I started referring clients to them and it's been very helpful for me.

As rewarding as it can feel when the ghost moves on, this work can also be frustrating and exhausting because you're dealing with souls who don't want to move on and start a new life.

I had an interesting thought as I was re-reading your letter and thinking about your strong desire to be a ghostbuster. Maybe, after a former life, you remained an earthbound spirit for a while and that's why you're so drawn to helping other souls cross over.

My brother had an unusual experience that left him feeling grateful he could do this work. He had a dream that a ghost entered his body so that he could feel what it was like to feel lost and stuck. I remember he called me as soon as he woke up and told me how awful it felt. It gave both of us a new perspective on the importance of our work.

The main thing you need to do is be patient and let your life plan unfold. If you continue to have this strong desire in your heart, you'll make a great ghostbuster when the time is right. If the desire leaves, that simply means you'll be called to do something else.

Referral to a Ghostbuster

Hello Ms. Bodine,

My wife and I just finished your book Relax, It's Only a Ghost *and enjoyed it a great deal. It's nice to know we are not alone. When we first moved into this house six years ago our two boys were convinced right away that we had ghosts. My wife and I disbelieved them at first but as time went on we too began to believe what they were saying was true. We have a feeling there are at least two souls stuck here and we are now very interested in their moving on. But I must admit to having a fear and feeling inept in helping them. I wouldn't want to screw things up.*

We are way out here in California and know this is a great distance for you to travel. We checked your ghostbuster listing but found none near us. Have you any suggestions to who, how, or what we can do? Your brief assistance would be greatly appreciated.

Greatest regards,

C & L M

Dear C & L M:

Unfortunately I often receive letters from people asking if I know of a reputable ghostbuster in their area and, needless to say, I don't always have someone to recommend. The best way to find a ghostbuster is through local referrals. I would suggest calling your local new age bookstore and asking if they know of someone they could refer you to. In the meantime, you can try asking the Squadron for help (see Solutions chapter) They're very effective (and always available!).

If you do find a good ghostbuster in your area, please let me know. Your letter has spurred me to set up a worldwide ghostbusters referral list at www.echobodine.com, my website.

Referral List

To all you reputable ghostbusters out there who don't charge an arm and a leg for your services (I've heard of some who charge in the thousands and that's ridiculous) would you mail or email me your name and a phone number or email address where people can reach you? Would you also share with me the methods you use to get rid of a ghost and how long you've been doing this work and your price? I'm going to post on my website a list of reputable ghostbusters all over the globe so that people can have someone to turn to, no matter where they live.

Chapter Fourteen

Solutions

*T*he letters I've shared here pretty well cover the gamut of ghost questions I'm asked. I hope you found them enlightening. I'm sure you noticed that in several of my responses I mentioned possible solutions, well, here are the six best solutions I know for dealing with earthbound spirits so that you're never victimized by them again. The great thing is, all of them can be used immediately whether you're a beginner or an experienced ghostbuster. They're simple, safe, and require only your intention to have things change.

The solution I recommend most often is the Clearing Exercise, so let's start there.

Clearing Exercise

One of the psychic gifts we are given is called Clairsentience, or the gift of sensing. What that means is that a clairsentient can walk into a room and feel the vibes. Can feel what other people are going through. Can sense through their body what's going on with other people. A lot of people have this gift and, because of it, they're walking around with others people's "stuff" all over them. The Clearing Exercise helps you get rid of this stuff. I think of it as a prayer or a request of the Universe. It's a very simple exercise. All you do is take a relaxing breath in and release it. Then ask God or the Universe silently or out loud to:

Please clear me.

Please clear me.

Take another calming breath in and out and ask:

Please clear my mind

Please clear my mind

Take another calming breath in and out and ask:

Please clear my body

Please clear my body

Take another calming breath in and out and ask:

Please clear my soul

Please clear my soul

Take another calming breath in and out and ask:

Please clear me psychically

Please clear me psychically.

You can use this same basic exercise for clearing your home, your office, your car, your children, other loved ones, or whatever feels or seems "off."

While it's very simple, it really works. You might think of it as a giant, invisible, energetic lint remover. You can do it as often as you want. If you are a particularly sensitive person, you might want to clear yourself whenever you've been around other people so that you don't carry their stuff around with you.

Burning Sage

This next solution involves burning the herb sage, which is a great "vibe cleanser." Some people believe that burning sage actually gets rid of ghosts, but it doesn't. It just gets the negative vibes out of the house, such as the anger, fear or hostility from the ghosts or from the people living in the house. The Native American Indians also suggest opening a window or door so that the smoke and the negative vibes have some place to go. Whenever I clear a house of ghosts, I always follow up by walking through the entire house with sage smoke. It makes the house feel squeaky clean on an energetic level!

I buy whole leaf Dalmation sage that has been crushed, but there are many different kinds on the market. You can grow it in your garden and in some places, you can pick it along the highway. Native American Indians suggest burning it in something made from the Earth. I didn't know this for a long time and burned it in a pie pan. It was still just as effective. But now I use an abalone shell. Just take about a fourth of a cup of sage, put it in the shell (or whatever) and light the sage. Once it catches on fire, gently blow it out. You actually want the smoke rather than the fire.

For those of you who haven't smelled sage before, I just want to warn you it smells (and looks like) marijuana.

While holding the container, walk through your house, asking God or the Universe to please clear your house of any negatives vibes or energy. I suggest that you use a feather to fan the smoke rather than directly blow on it because you might blow too hard and get sparks flying all over, which is not safe. You also want to be mindful of smoke detectors when walking around a house carrying something smoking.

Air Freshener

This next solution might sound pretty silly, but it's actually proven to be quite effective. If your child thinks there are ghosts or "monsters" in their room or somewhere else in the house, go out and buy a can of air freshener. Show your child the can and tell him or her to let you know the next time they see the ghost

When your child comes to tell you they see the ghost, show them how to spray the freshener at the ghost while telling it to leave and go to Heaven *now*. Be sure to sound firm so your child understands that if ghosts are given very clear directions, they *will* leave. Our kids need to get the message loud and clear that there is something they can do if they see ghosts. They should never have to feel like victims of mischievous ghosts!

I've recommended this to many parents and gotten lots of letters back telling me that they tried this and it worked, so give it a try the next time your little one complains about the "monster" in his room.

The Squadron

If you suspect you have a ghost, it may be time to call in the Squadron. My spirit guides first taught me about these guys. They are a bunch of former ghosts who have moved on to the other side. They decided to form a group to help stuck souls go home. Of course they make house calls!

I usually recommend that you call on the Squadron at night because all of the activity in the home has calmed down and they can come in and do their work when everyone's sleeping. Once they've come and gone (you can assume if you've asked for their help that they'll be there) ask for a healing angel to come in and fill up your house with white light of blessings and protection. Also ask them to seal the house up so that you won't be bothered by more intruders.

The biggest problem with this solution is that people don't believe the Squadron will really come to *their* house. They don't believe it's possible. Believe me, they have come every time I've called on them, and they know their stuff. It works.

Prayer for Protection

Finally, I think everyone should have a good prayer for protection. My psychic development teacher always used to say that if we ever felt scared by ghost or spirit activity, we should say a prayer that made us feel safe. Here's one I learned from the Unity Church, but of course you can use any prayer you like:

The Light of God surrounds me
The Love of God enfolds me
The Power of God protects me
The Presence of God watches over me
Wherever I am,
God is.
And all is well.

In Closing

In closing I would like to say that we attract experiences to us that will help us (our souls) grow. If you have attracted ghosts to you, try to step back from the experience and look at it objectively. Look at how this experience might help you to grow in some area of your life. No experience in our life is a waste of our time. Look for the gem, the gift in the experience, that might help you heal some issue, might help enhance your self-worth, might help you feel more empowered.

This is what life is all about, creating situations to help us heal. So pay attention and remember: You are more powerful than any ghost or spirit. You never have to be victimized by any of these earthbound souls, but it will always be up to you as to how it goes.

God Bless.

Echo Bodine

Recommended Book List

I have written several books that can provide solutions for you depending upon your needs:

If you're interested in learning about spiritual, laying on hands healing, I recommend *Hands That Heal* (ACS Publications).

If you would like to learn more about your soul's perspective on life, death and life after death, I recommend *Echoes of the Soul* (New World Library).

If you would like to learn about how to live by your intuition, I recommend *A Still Small Voice: A Psychic's Guide to Awakening Intuition* (New World Library).

If you would like to read more about ghosts and how to get rid of them, I recommend *Relax, It's Only a Ghost* (Fair Winds Press).

And if you would like to understand and develop your psychic abilities, I recommend my new book coming out January, 2003, called *A Gift: Understanding and Developing Your Psychic Abilities* (New World Library).

Here are some other great books I recommend:

The Eagle and the Rose A fascinating spiritual adventure, by Rosemary Altea. Warner Vision Books. 1 800-759-0190, ISBN 0-446-60364-3, Also available on audio cassette.

Proud Spirit: Lessons, Insights and Healing From the "Voice of the Spirit World", by Rosemary Altea. Eagle Brook Morrow, ISBN 0-688-16067-0

You Own The Power: Stories and Exercises to Inspire and Unleash the Force Within, by Rosemary Altea. HarperCollins, ISBN 0060959363, also available on audiocassette

Forever Ours by coroner, Janis Amatuzio. In her book she explores the mysterious realm of visions, experiences and communications experienced by families at the threshold of the deaths of their loved ones ... You can order the book through Midwest Forensic Pathology P.A., Phone 763-236-9050, fax 763-236-9051, 3960 Coon Rapids Blvd. Coon Rapids, MN55433

Children's Past Lives, How Past Life Memories Affect Your Child, by Carol Bowman. Bantam Books, ISBN 0-553-57485-X

Return from Heaven, Beloved Relatives Reincarnate Within Your Family, by Carol Bowman. HarperCollins, ISBN 006-019-5711

Haunted Places, The National Directory, Ghostly Abodes, Sacred Sites, UFO Landings, Supernatural Locations, by Dennis

William Hauck. Penguin Books, ISBN 0-14-025734-9 (sorted by state)

The International Directory of Haunted Places, Ghostly Abodes, Sacred Sites, And Other Supernatural Locations, by Dennis William Hauck. Penguin Books, ISBN 0-14-029635-2 (sorted by country)

Great American Ghost Stories, by Hans Holzer. Barnes & Noble Books, ISBN 0-7607-2733-3

More Where The Ghosts Are, The Ultimate Guide to Haunted Houses, by Hans Holzer. Citadel Press, ISBN 0-8065-2219-4

Life Beyond, Compelling Evidence for Past Lives and Existence After Death, by Hans Holzer. Contemporary Books, ISBN 0-8092-3577-3

The Lively Ghosts of Ireland, by Hans Holzer. Dorset Press, ISBN 0-7607-2733

True Encounters with the World Beyond, by Hans Holzer. Black Dog & Leventhal Publishers, ISBN 1884822649

True Ghost Stories, by Hans Holzer. Dorset Press, ISBN 0-7607-27341

Hans Holzer's Travel Guide To Haunted Houses, by Hans Holzer & Nathan Frerichs. Black Dog and Leventhal Publishers, Inc. ISBN 1579120164

We Are Not Forgotten, George Anderson's Messages of Love and Hope From the Other Side, by Joel Martin and Patricia Romanowski. Putnam Berkeley, ISBN 0-425-13288-9

George Anderson's We Don't Die, George Anderson's Conversations With The Other Side by Joel Martin and Patricia Romanowski. Putnam Berkeley, ISBN 0-425-11451

Lessons From the Light, Extraordinary Messages of Comfort and Hope from the Other Side, by George Anderson and Andrew Barone. Putnam Berkeley, ISBN 0-425-17416-6

Walking in The Garden of Souls, Advice From the Hereafter for Living in the Here and Now, by George Anderson and Andrew Barone. Putnam, ISBN 0-399-14790-X

Sixth Sense of Children: Nurturing Your Child's Intuitive Abilities, by Litany Burns. New American Library, ISBN 0451205251

The Psychic Pathway, A Workbook for Reawakening the Voice of Your Soul, by Sonia Choquette, Ph.D., Three Rivers Press. ISBN 0-517-88407-0

One Last Time. A psychic medium speaks to those we have loved and lost, by John Edward. Includes a workbook section to help you tune into your own psychic abilities. Putnam Berkeley, ISBN 0-425-16692-9

How to Develop Your Sixth Sense: A practical guide to developing your extraordinary powers, by David Lawson. Thorsons Publishing, ISBN 0-00-711700-0

Questions from Earth, Answers from Heaven, A Psychic's Intuitive Discussion of Life, Death, and What Awaits Us Beyond, by Char Margolis with Victoria St. George. St. Martins Press ISBN 0312241992

"A World Beyond" The First Eyewitness Account of the Hereafter From the World-famous Psychic Arthur Ford, by Ruth Montgomery. Fawcett Crest, ISBN 0-449-20832-X

"The World To Come" The Guides Long-Awaited Predictions for the Dawning Age, by Ruth Montgomery. Harmony Books, ISBN 0-609-60479-1

"Search For The Truth" by Ruth Montgomery. Fawcett Crest Books, ISBN 0-449-21085-5

How to Communicate with Spirits, by Elizabeth Owens. Llewellyn, ISBN 1-56718-530-4

Be Your Own Psychic, by Doris T. Patterson and Violet M. Shelley. Based on the Edgar Cayce Readings. Edgar Cayce Foundation. ISBN 87604-079-2

Awakening Your Psychic Powers. An Edgar Cayce Guide. Open your inner mind and control your psychic intuition, by Henry Reed, Ph.D. St. Martin's Paperbacks. ISBN 0-312-95868-4

You are Psychic! An MIT-trained scientist's proven program for expanding your psychic powers, by Pete A. Sanders, Jr. Fawcett Books, ISBN 0-449-90507-1

Talking to Heaven A medium's message of life after death, by James Van Praagh. Dutton Penguin Group, ISBN 0-525-94268-8

Reaching to Heaven A spiritual journey through life and death, by James Van Praagh. Dutton Penguin Group. ISBN 0-525-94481-8

Heaven and Earth Making the psychic connection, by James Van Praagh. Simon & Schuster ISBN 0-7432-2358-6, also available on audio cassette.

Audio Cassettes

Developing Your Own Psychic Powers by John Edward. A 6-tape Audio Program. Hay House. www.hayhouse.com, 1-800-654-5126